The Telemarketing Handbook

The Telemarketing Handbook

Pauline Marks
Chairman of Audiotext Plc

Business Books

Copyright © 1989 Pauline Marks

First published in Great Britain in 1989 by
Business Books Limited
An imprint of Century Hutchinson Ltd
Brookmount House, 62–65 Chandos Place, Covent Garden,
London WC2N 4NW

Century Hutchinson Australia (Pty) Ltd
89–91 Albion Street, Surry Hills, New South Wales 2010

Century Hutchinson New Zealand Ltd
PO Box 40–086, 32–34 View Road, Glenfield, Auckland 10, New Zealand

Century Hutchinson South Africa (Pty) Ltd
PO Box 337, Bergvlei 2012, South Africa

Typeset by Deltatype Ltd, Ellesmere Port
Printed and Bound by Mackays of Chatham PLC,
Chatham, Kent

British Library Cataloguing in Publication Data

Marks, Pauline
    The telemarketing handbook.
    1. Salesmanship. Use of telephones – Manuals
    I. Title II. Marks, Pauline. The telephone marketing book
    658.8'12

ISBN 0–09–1742188

To Martin, my PR man for 35 years

Contents

1

The telephone marketing explosion

The telephone marketing explosion has happened. Every single person in the Western world is involved as amazing new technology is integrated into business and consumer functions, with creative new applications being discovered almost every day. And it's all happened rapidly since the winter day in 1958 when HM the Queen dialled the first STD call to begin a period of the most dramatic radical reform since the acquisition of the National Telephone Company in 1912.

Prime Minister Margaret Thatcher also made history in October 1983 when, out of up to 100 million radio listeners, twelve astonished callers spoke to her directly in a phone-in programme. All the lines into the BBC's studio were jammed with calls for nearly two hours before the programme began.

Two years later, innovative telephone fund-raising on a massive scale was carried out around the world, linked to the 'Live Aid' concerts. The pledges made in this way accounted for a major part of the $49 million raised.

'Dial-A-Shuttle' telephone lines were set up in the USA, so that nearly a quarter million callers could listen in to the astronauts talking in the Challenger space shuttle prior to its doomed last flight. Introduced by A.T. & T. in 1980, the system meant that 8,000 callers at any one minute could listen at a cost of 50¢ for the first minute and 35¢ for each additional minute, plus tax. The scheme was not without its critics. Callers were not at all pleased to find that they were also paying to hear half minute ads incorporated every five minutes thanking American Airlines, Quality Inns and Tang for their sponsorship of the phone-in programme.

It was in the USA that the Scotsman Alexander Graham Bell invented the telephone and it was there that phone-selling was born. A few of the American agencies tried to export it lock stock and barrel to Europe, on the assumption that anything that worked in the USA ought to work in Europe as well. But, as

1

many direct response marketers had previously found, it was not possible to transport marketing techniques without making substantial adjustments for the different attitudes, needs and response mechanisms of the individual country. A certain amount of modification is always needed. Coca Cola may now be almost universal, but the ways in which 'Coke' is sold needs everywhere to be distinct.

So it came about that, although the Americans were the forerunners of telephone marketing, ways had to be found of adapting rather than adopting existing methods. It was soon apparent that, although the American citizen received, and now expected, a certain amount of pressurized high-powered selling over the phone, his European counterpart, new to phone-selling, was completely averse to receiving hard-sell solicitations. Having said this, it was also apparent that the Europeans were not in any way averse to receiving telephone calls providing that they were politely and justifiably structured.

Britain followed the US closely in the field of serious telephone marketing, but the Germans and French swiftly saw the value in this new medium, and quickly began their own industries – followed in quick succession by the Scandinavian countries, Benelux, Switzerland and the rest of the world.

In Sri Lanka, for example, the World Bank reported that, after telephones were installed in several villages, the farmers began selling their produce at 85 per cent of its price in Colombo. Before the telephones were installed, produce was selling at 55 per cent of the Colombo price.

In China, people regard the personal telephone as a status symbol, with just three million instruments for a billion people.

It is no surprise to learn, therefore, that researchers from the Brookings Institution, the University of Texas and Stanford University have found that a one per cent rise in the number of telephones over one hundred people between 1950 and 1955 contributed to a rise in per capita income of about three per cent in the period from 1955 to 1962 (see Figure 1).

Why the explosion had to occur

Telephone marketing was slow to take hold in Europe until

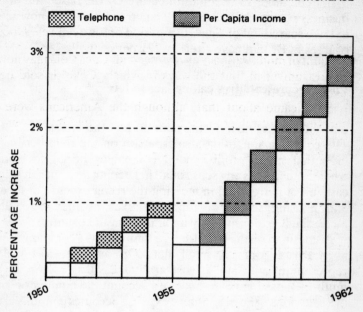

Figure 1 Comparison of telephone increase/per capita income increase

1973. In January of that year the price of a barrel of oil stood at $2.59 – about the price of a Perrier in the Ritz hotel today. In October of that year the Yom Kippur War erupted in the Middle East, and the Organization of Petroleum Exporting Countries (OPEC) doubled the price of that barrel to $5.17. Two months later OPEC raised the price again, this time to a whopping $11.65 a barrel, an increase of almost 450 per cent in one year. Everything began to cost much more because manufacturing, processing and distribution industries all require energy – and the cost of energy in all forms was rising sharply as a consequence of oil price increases.

The advertising and marketing industry was profoundly affected. Media advertising costs, like other business costs, sky-rocketed. For example, a full-page colour advertisement in *The Observer* now costs £27,500 in contrast to £2,950 in 1975 – an increase of 932 per cent.

In September 1975, a month before OPEC raised the prices, business postage bills also spiralled upwards, and by now seems to have soared out of sight. In a period of fourteen years, postal charges in Britain have risen by 271 per cent.

Cost of representatives calling face to face

It wasn't, however, only in media advertising and direct mail that the marketing industry came to feel the effects of OPEC. The cost of maintaining a salesperson on the road became so high that many profit-minded companies began to wonder whether there was any sense at all in keeping fleets of salesmen's cars full of petrol, and in meeting the rising expense of feeding and housing scores of representatives as they went their increasingly expensive way up and down the country.

A salesman on the road for a year now costs a company almost as much as does a small flat. On average, a travelling representative is said to cost around £29,000 a year. If you multiply those figures to take into account the number of 'reps' in a sales force, the horrendous expense becomes painfully clear. If you then divide that expense by the number of customers even the most energetic salesperson is capable of seeing in one day, then the cost per call becomes difficult to swallow and almost impossible to digest. Finally, if you divide the expense involved by the number of sales actually 'closed', then the cost per sale can often reach absurd proportions, especially if relatively low-price items are involved.

Sending salespeople out on the road has, in many cases, simply become a luxury. Worse, it may actually be a hopelessly antiquated technique for many companies; one which ought now to be dispensed with as being lackadaisical and ineffective. Every further day salespeople are kept on the road results in costs continuing to rise and a lessening of profits.

Total personalization

Telephone selling can and does replace the old-fashioned inefficient, horse-and-buggy approach. This new method ensures instant access to a customer, costs pennies rather than

Telephone selling can and does replace the old-fashioned inefficient horse-and-buggy approach.

pounds, and lends itself to a flexible marketing strategy based on sound market research.

In short, the telephone is the most obvious sales tool of the modern age, an instrument we use throughout all our working days for every kind of purpose, and which we cannot afford to ignore when we devise our marketing strategies. All this is not new of course. Many successful companies have included telephone marketing as an integral part of their marketing mix for years. These include such household names as Walls Ice Cream, Bird's Eye Foods, EMI records, IBM, Britvic, Time Life Books and Rank Xerox. There is no doubt that, subject to circumstances, telephone selling can do a better job, for less, than any other sales medium that exists.

Increase profitability without increasing overheads

This headline is everybody's dream. It sounds too good to be true. Can one cut costs and increase results by releasing resources? The answer is yes. All the ingredients are there. Working on the axiom that the more contacts you make the more orders you receive, a telephone marketing promotion can swiftly completely cover an entire field of prospects for the product or service being offered.

As an example, let us look at the retail newsagents' trade. There are approximately 41,365 retail newsagent outlets in the UK. Necessarily they have to stock a very wide range of merchandise, and therefore they are probably subjected to more sales calls than most other retailers. While the shopkeeper may very well welcome a salesman's visit during off-peak periods when perhaps he is bored and glad of an opportunity to chat, it is different when the representative is standing in front of his counter taking up valuable space to make his sales pitch – to the detriment of the paying customers who are waiting to be served. Often the irritation this situation causes a shopkeeper results in the representative being sent away empty-handed, when the merchandise is in fact needed to replace out-of-stock items.

Timing is very important. Based on the proviso that an average salesman can call on ten to 12 outlets a day, it would need a salesforce of 115 people in order to cover all the retail newsagent outlets once every six weeks.

If, during the interim period, a salesman from a competing manufacturer visits the retailer, perhaps at the very moment his stock levels are low in the particular merchandise, it is quite likely that the rival company will receive the order from the retailer – who does not maintain high enough stock levels.

Had, however, that same retailer received a regular weekly telephone call, without doubt that same order would have been placed with the regular company. As a further rationalization of this point, consider the fact that a face-to-face salesman making his ten to 12 calls daily would not expect to receive an order from each prospect he visited. An optimistic salesman would perhaps consider he could make 25 per cent sales. Therefore, taking the average salary as £29,000 (plus) per annum, each sale will cost his company betwen £40 and £45. In this context it must immediately make good sense to use the telephone to obtain repeat orders where the product/merchandise is well known and the customer is fully aware of the range available. This does not mean that all a telephone communicator has to do is to call and ask if the prospect would like to repeat a previous order. The communicator should upsell to an equal, or greater, extent than the face-to-face salesman. After all, he has a great advantage. He is not standing in front of the counter or desk taking up valuable floor space; and most of all he has the undivided attention of the customer at the other end of the telephone.

Releasing resources through lead generation

Qualification by telephone marketing should be an integral part of marketing plans. The savings realized in making full use of an expensive salesperson's time are substantial. If every call he makes is now to a definitely potential customer, then his order rate must increase and the overall sales (and profitability) improve. The cost of making the telephone call in this context is insignificant, particularly if the same call is used not only to provide a firm qualified lead, but also to obtain other relevant information which can help.

By releasing the resource of trained salespeople, they can now be employed to do the job for which they are best qualified – opening up new accounts, and servicing major customers who justify such attention and will respond by placing more substantial business.

The facts

The telephone communicator works in a relaxed, friendly environment, unhampered by rain, snow, sleet, heatwaves, car troubles or the other problems with which the travelling company salesman is beset.

Four telephones, manned by trained communicators for six

hours daily, for a five-day working week, fifty weeks in the year, can effectively be expected to produce between 35,000 and 40,000 sales calls a year.

The telephone can stand alone, but when it is used in conjunction with other media of mass communication, it will very sharply increase the effectiveness of each approach – either as a direct selling tool, a back-up to other forms of advertising such as off-the-page mail order, or for market research needed to find the names and addresses of prospective customers. I would stress here, as I do later in this book, that market research should never be used as a guise for selling – and the prospects on the other end of the telephone must always be told the purpose and reason for the call at the beginning of the approach, rather than at the end.

Used correctly, and ethically, information gained will quickly allow informed decisions to be taken on whether an expensive face-to-face salesperson should call. Moreover, it will frequently open the door for the salesman in those instances where he has previously been unable to gain entry.

Why is it that a skilled telephone communicator can make contact when a face-to-face salesperson is unable to do so?

Most of us are unskilled at 'getting rid of people' who we think are likely to be time-wasters. This is often particularly true of the small local retailer, insurance broker, estate agent or other service seller, whose reputation has been built on the friendly relations and good humour he extends to all comers. An unexpected salesperson who enters his premises is often, in a sense, an unknown quantity – the prospect simply cannot tell in advance how much time that person will take up, and subsequently he is not very willing to start a dialogue with him. The telephone is different. If the businessman is really not interested he will say so; if he is busy, he will not hesitate to agree to being called back at a later time that he designates; if he intends to place an order he can do so quickly and efficiently with the minimum of delay. He does not need to give a great deal of time to the transaction. This can be summed up by the following fact:

When the telephone rings, we all give it our immediate and full attention, no matter what; yet, when a sales representative calls upon us, we will interrupt his sales pitch to go and answer the phone.

There is no doubt which method of direct contact gets top priority treatment everywhere, and at all times.

The marriage of direct mail and phoneselling

With the high cost of postage, print and mailing house charges, sending information through the mail is costly. Sending it out 'cold' to an unknown list can at times be very wasteful, since it isn't until the responses come in that a company can gauge which of the recipients were likely to be interested in the first place. A mailing list of 1,000 home-owners, for example, doesn't tell us much about their interest in buying swimming pools; it only shows that they own their homes and do so within a certain locality which is a prime area for swimming pool ownership. Turning that same list over to experienced telephone communicators will produce more positive information. By skilled probing, they will reduce that list of 1,000 home-owners to those who are truly interested, allowing the expensive mailing pieces to be sent only to those people who are likely to study the literature with the attention it needs, if the reader is to be converted into a buyer.

A pre-advertising telephone campaign will tell a company whether or not the name and address file it is holding is that of likely prospects; it also provides a valuable personal contact with the potential buyer establishing his needs and identifying particular areas of interest before the brochure and letter are put in the post.

Continuing to examine the marketing requirements of the swimming pool manufacturer as a case in point. It is obvious that his segmentation of the marketplace is necessarily small, and very difficult to pinpoint in a mailing list. An introductory call therefore, in a pre-advertising campaign, would include something along the lines of:

As a homeowner, Mr X, I wonder whether you have a fairly large garden?

After all, if the man does not have a large garden, what would he be doing with a swimming pool?

Gerry Broidy, the man who did a great deal to develop telephone marketing internationally for Time-Life, once told me that, as part of Time-Life's training to its communicators selling books, they had a large printed notice in the department which stated:

If the man says he doesn't read, thank him for his time and cease the call.

We have always followed this maxim. If the basic need for the product or service is not there, it is economically essential that communicators cease the call courteously – and sooner, rather than later.

Our swimming pool campaigner would perhaps continue by commenting:

If you don't already own a swimming pool, I am sure you would be interested in hearing more about the new XYZ heated swimming pool, and about the increased value it adds to your house, Mr X.

Hearing about the increased value should encourage Mr X to immediately express an interest in the proposal – or, of course, he could say 'No' right away. If he does say 'No' it is up to the communicator to probe the reason for the negative response – it could be money, no swimmers in the family, age or just a total lack of interest in owning a pool. The well-trained communicator will be able to evaluate the quality of the response received, and by carefully continuing the dialogue will be able to designate the prospect as justifying further expense by dispatching him a mailing, or having his name and address removed from the prospect file for the product.

Direct mail in a follow-up situation to a telephone call is thus carefully targeted with the minimum of wastage. Once the literature has been sent (and checks made to confirm it has been received) a further telephone call may be made to verify that the recipient is a firm qualified 'lead' and an appointment made for a salesperson to call.

Whether one is selling a swimming pool, or a piece of capital equipment, the technique works consistently well. It can be used to renew subscriptions, re-open lapsed accounts, and sell just about anything. As an indication of the success you may expect, consider the fact that two telephone calls (pre- and post-mailing) enabled us to sell a £30,000 crane directly without even the need for a face-to-face salesperson's visit!

Flexibility of testing

Media advertising campaigns are, of course, the brain children of creative advertising agency people, but whether they work or not must often necessarily be left to chance. Once an advertisement is placed in a magazine reaching thousands of readers, the deed is done. Each reader is exposed to the same sales message, whether it is likely to motivate them as an individual or not, or in money terms, whether it is cost-effective or wasteful. The budget has been allocated, and, all too often, the cash involved goes down the drain.

This is not the case with telephone selling. Flexibility is the keynote here. You do not have to stay with failure when you use this medium. Scripts can be changed daily, or even hourly, approaches can be altered, and then altered again, as often as necessary until a cost-effective sales pitch is evolved and seen to be working.

No one is perfect; no one in the marketing business can justifiably claim to know exactly what arguments will sway most buyers, unless extensive market research is undertaken. For this to be tried with print advertising or radio/TV commercials, is extremely costly. It means running ads with different approaches one after the other, until the accepted version is found. The creative and production costs are usually prohibitive.

In telephone selling, production costs are very small by comparison, and test marketing of various approaches can be measured in very few pounds.

Six different sales approaches can, for example, be tested on 100 prospects each, and the results can then be carefully compared for a cost of probably not more than £3,000. If approach A proves three times as effective as any of the other tests, then approach A can be used with confidence right across the board, and a profitable campaign can be launched. One might find that different campaigns work equally well, but for different target groups. You could obtain better results in the south with one test and the other could prove more effective in the north. In telephone selling, a company pays only for what it uses, but it must make quite sure that only the best possible approach is made through serious testing of all the possibilities.

As a general rule, we find that a carefully qualified test of 100 contacts is adequate to validate the success of each script, and that, providing sufficient communicators are available, educated assessments are possible in just one day. No other medium can equal this test flexibility in terms of both speed and low cost.

2
Making sure your telephone marketing department is cost-effective

Don't run away with the idea that telephone marketing *must* be cost-effective. This is often far from the case, and many large company managers who boast about the sales achieved by their telephone departments have not really evaluated the true costs. The best way to ensure that what you are achieving is a profit is to sit down and look at the two types of costs: the tangible and the intangible. These should be worked out on an hourly rate.

The tangible costs should include:

Overhead factor, square footage, lighting, heating, wear and tear of equipment
Telephone rentals
Telephone charges (calculated on meter units)
Communicator fees
Supervisory and management fees
List research
Printing
Clerical assistance.

Intangible could include:

Setting-up costs
Bonuses and incentives
Scriptwriting and re-writes
Involvement of management
Briefing.

Allowance must be made for the variable factors in telephone marketing: for example, the number of telephone meter units used will vary with time of day, area to which call is being made and length of time taken. The important equation to make is

$$\frac{\text{Cost per telephone hour}}{\text{Number of sales}} = \text{Profit}$$

In Chapter 4, I have detailed recording systems and the logic for their use. These are logical not only in that they provide the information you require for costing but they also can easily be maintained and read by the manager and supervisors in terms of individual achievement.

Each communicator hour must be detailed in a controlled and careful way, and the records should be evaluated daily/weekly/ monthly in comparison with previous reports so that any deterioration in achievements is easily recognized. If everyone in the department dials three given calls one day, this can quickly become the accepted call pattern unless charts and records are not only maintained but evaluated regularly.

Targets should be based upon the achievements of the most successful communicator, always bearing in mind your hourly cost. The telephone manager must be made aware of the *minimum* sales required for profitability as well of course as the *target* figure. Where this is exceeded, there should be incentives given ceremoniously to the communicators, and less obviously but still tangibly to the supervisor involved.

We're here to make a profit

In our experience telephone sales managers often lose sight of the fact that they are in business for *profit* and that the records have to reflect this hour by hour rather than on a weekly or monthly basis. Weeks and months are too late for improvement in telephone selling and the manager's plans for the next day's approach to his or her staff must be based upon the results in front of him for the previous six or seven hours' work. It is the manager's responsibility to make any necessary alterations to see that the maximum profit is made per working hour by correcting inefficiencies or ineptitudes which are obvious from the records.

The first one or two days of any operation must be discounted. This is the intangible setting-up cost. It can take up to ten working communicator hours to find the right level of approach; the script must be adjusted as necessary – maybe by altering the basic offer or producing alternative answers to objections which are being raised.

Response hours vary

In consumer promotions the records will indicate at which hours of the day the prospect is most likely to be at home to answer the telephone as well as the hours to avoid, namely, when it is very difficult to get permission for a full presentation to be made, although the telephone was answered. This depends upon the category of consumer approached; parents of young children are usually harassed between 5 and 7.30 pm and not responsive to any sort of sales presentations. Working couples are busy preparing and eating a meal and have the same attitude to callers at this time. Retired people, on the other hand, will often respond more satisfactorily at this hour than if they were to be interrupted during their favourite TV programmes.

Business call contact rates vary according to the job title of the person you are trying to reach and the type of company he/she represents. In my experience the higher echelon of management should not be approached either on Monday mornings or Friday afternoons. Middle management, on the other hand, are often more receptive at these times.

These are all facts that well-maintained records will indicate and allow the manager to alter his calling patterns so that any non-profitable hours are eliminated from the daily schedule, and to increase sales by engaging more communicators to cover those hours in the day that prove most profitable.

Improve or remove

The achievements of the most successful communicators should be used as the next day's target, but in a well-controlled telephone sales department there should not be more than 15 per cent difference between the best and the least successful operator (excluding new staff) and the telephone manager must always remember the golden rule:

Don't carry dead weight. A consistent low level reduces the cost-effectiveness of the whole department.

It is so easy to think, 'I am sure he/she will improve. I'll wait another day before I ask him/her to leave.' That other day is one too many. Successful telephone communicators are competitive. They are encouraged to be so. If everybody around them is making constantly successful calls, they too are keen; when, however, a slow and inadequate colleague is nearby, their own pace and results slacken. No department manager should hesitate to remove the offenders: they knew what was required of them when attending the initial interview and this has been emphasized at training sessions.

Communicators, not clerks

My pet aversion is the term 'telesales'. People who work in telephone marketing are communicators. This exactly explains their job function. And because they are employed to communicate, or in simpler terms, to paint word pictures, they must not be mis-employed for other purposes such as undertaking the nitty-gritty of the clerical work which goes hand in hand with telephone marketing.

Basic information should, whenever possible, be pre-prepared and made available prior to a campaign. Handing over a sheet from the Yellow Pages makes the job laborious and tedious. Using data prep operators or clerks to make lists available in an easily readable format allows the communicators to amend the records where necessary, and write down the information while they are actually talking on the telephone.

Increasing your 'talk' time, increases your profitability

To help things along the way, it is essential to encourage communicators to wear headsets. However, it must be said that most managers report a marked aversion on the part of their staff to use the headsets. Once upon a time there was good reason: the equipment available was cumbersome to use, and inevitably messed up hairstyles. Nowadays there are feather-light under-the-chin models with detachable ear-tips for easy cleaning.

Hands-free operation means that communicators can write notes or enter data into a computer, turn over pages in a script and operate altogether more efficiently. Furthermore, distracting outside noises are mostly eliminated. Use of a headset can increase efficiency by more than 25 per cent.

Computers

A micro is now so inexpensive that it is well worth providing communicators with screens, and having a programme prepared which will, as far as possible, allow for the operator to punch in maximum information using minimum codes.

Figure 2

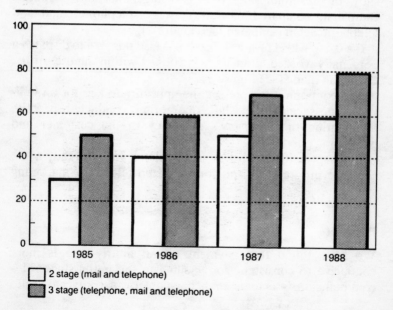

2 stage (mail and telephone)

3 stage (telephone, mail and telephone)

Figure 3 Sample letter

Mrs Brown   Sabra Travel
211 Creighton Avenue,
Brighton, BN2 1RJ

Dear Mrs Brown,
Thank you for talking to me on the telephone today.
   We are most appreciative of your interest in our exciting package tours, and immediately enclose a brochure so that you may lose no time in re-booking with us – and avoiding any possible surcharges.
   SABRA Travel are quick to appreciate the value of your interest, and you can be assured of the same keen attention at all times.
   Yours sincerely,
   G. Gould (Director)

To avoid errors, a single line of data at a time can appear on the screen, followed by validation. A competent programmer will ensure that the codes allowed maximize the possibility of detecting errors by building in check points.

Using such a simple system, and combining it with a plotter, you can obtain an end-result which will provide both pie-charts and histograms, and produce graphs which could, for example, show the resultant sales of a two-stage mail and telephone campaign, compared to a three-stage telephone, mail and telephone again campaign (see Figure 2).

If a daisy-wheel printer is used, it is also possible to dispatch a personally worded letter to each contact within minutes of the call being made (see Figure 3).

The communicator presses the appropriate key for an individual message and the whole operation is conducted speedily, highlighting the company's efficiency to the customer and generating goodwill.

In Chapter 10 I discuss in greater detail various ready-made software programmes and computerized telephone marketing systems.

Payment

We have found that payment on an hourly rate is more conducive to consistent good selling in the initial stages of a communicator's employ than payment on a contact or sales commission scheme. Many good people who would have made excellent communicators are at first frightened at the thought of working on anything other than a flat rate, and others, not so naturally successful, are possibly tempted to falsify their record sheets if they are getting paid only on results. In 'Audiotext' we find that a guaranteed fair standard wage initially gives confidence to the operator, who may then progress to bonuses and incentives, and occasionally be offered opportunities of working on a per-contact/sales success rate of pay scheme where he can prove his proficiency in the telephone selling skills that have been developed. Again, this must be reflected in your hourly rate costs and be dependent upon your profit margin ratio to each sale made.

3

How and when to choose and make good use of a telephone marketing bureau

Before deciding to use an agency you must establish your marketing objectives and put together your marketing plan. Choose a bureau, rather than endeavour to set up in-house, if your needs stack up against the following:

1. You intend to conduct fragmented campaigns, each with individual sales needs.
2. You need intensive volume calling on an infrequent basis.
3. There is insufficient availability of telephone hardware to handle your possible requirements.
4. The telephone marketing is required urgently, and must be undertaken by highly trained communicators.
5. The project is one which needs to be tested before you proceed on a roll out basis either in-house or with the agency.
6. You need to demonstrate that applying telephone marketing to your product or service will prove efficacious.
7. There is a gap in representation. If you don't have a locum to fill a situation when the area representative has left, is on holiday or sick leave, the bureau can work quickly and efficiently to take orders and keep the area 'warm' until a salesperson can make his usual visits. My bureau has frequently been called in to a situation where a senior representative of a large specialist manufacturing company has suddenly left the job and gone over to the competition. By prompt action on the part of the manufacturer in approaching our bureau, we have been able to telephone every existing customer before the wayward ex-employee has got into his car and started to poach their business for his new company.

How do you go about it? Plunge in straightaway, and base your choice on the lowest quotation, or choose an agency because the sales manager is an amiable fellow, or a pretty girl, who seems to know what he or she is talking about – or do you probe further?

Firstly evaluate the sales manager's pitch.

Experience

A new broom may sweep clean, but an older one has been broken in and should certainly do a better job.

Check whether the bureau has experience in handling similar requirements to your own. Ask to see examples of the scripts used (in non-competing situations), and request a list of references. Don't be satisfied with one or two names. An agency in the business for more than two years should be able to provide a list of at least 20 clients for you to choose two or three names at random. Ask for details of the percentage of repeat business obtained and whether or not the bureau is involved in any repetitive or 'roll out' situations, i.e., where the client is so satisfied with the initial results he asks the bureau to continue on a large scale.

Size of bureau

A key question is 'Are your telephones all in use every day?' rather than 'How many telephones do you have?' A large installation does not necessarily mean a successful bureau – just that they have a great many telephones. Obviously, if the set-up comprizes fewer than 25 telephones, think carefully before continuing. It could be that there are excellent reasons for such a small unit – or alternatively they could be unused to handling substantial volumes and will have problems in providing you with sufficient capacity. Telephone marketing is a numbers game, and a very competitive one. Four communicators working in a team will usually produce better results for you than two communicators working for twice the length of time. The very small bureau will probably cost less initially, but may well prove more expensive in the long run in relation to results achieved.

Marketing know-how

A good bureau will want to ask you a lot of questions too. Experience should provide them with the ability to hold an in-depth discussion on the place for the telephone in your particular marketing mix, and its economic viability for your specific purpose. They will need to know about your products, marketing methods and salesforce. A successful bureau will probably ask for a profile of your average customer, and should insist on a test of the scheme before allowing you to proceed with the whole campaign.

If the bureau is able to advise cogently on new list creation this is a plus when you are seeking to enlarge your customer base through cold calling.

British Direct Marketing Association guidelines

The British Direct Marketing Association (BDMA) founded a telephone committee at my instigation in 1982. Bureau members of the telephone committee are not necessarily the best in the business, nor are non-members unworthy by default. All it means in effect is that members have agreed to subscribe to the guidelines laid down by the Association which ensure that calls are handled to a very high standard of courtesy and care. It is very worthwhile checking to see if the proposed company is a member – or if they set themselves certain standards. The BDMA is located at: Grosvenor Gardens House, Grosvenor Gardens, London SW1W 0BS, Telephone: 01 630 7322, and they will gladly provide a list of members. I do recommend that you place a copy of the guidelines in any area in which your in-house telephone marketing is located.

BDMA Guidelines

Introduction

The British Direct Marketing Association Guidelines for Telephone Marketing Practices are intended to provide organisations involved in direct Telephone Marketing to both *Consumers* and *Businesses* with principles of ethical and professional conduct.

All members of the BDMA shall comply with any relevant legislation which may supersede these guidelines. In addition, all members shall comply with the following guidelines in respect of activities not covered by specific law, or when legal requirements are less restrictive than the guidelines.

Disclosure

1. The name of the company on whose behalf a sales and marketing call is made or received should be voluntarily and promptly disclosed, and this information repeated on request at any time during the conversation.

2. The purpose of the call should be made clear at the start, and the content of the call should be restricted to matters directly relevant to its purpose.

3. The name, address and telephone number of the company responsible for the call should appear in the telephone directory, or be available through directory enquiries, or be readily available through another source. This information shall also be given on request.

4. If a telephone marketer is acting as an agent of a company, the name, address and telephone number of the agent should be disclosed upon request at any time during the conversation.

5. If a person phoned was recommended by a third party, the identity of the third party should be voluntarily and promptly disclosed.

Honesty

1. Telephone marketers should not evade the truth or deliberately mislead. Any questions should be answered honestly and fully to the best of the knowledge available.

2. Sales and marketing calls should not be executed in the guise of research or a survey. In cases where the words 'research' or 'survey' are used the information obtained must not be used to form the basis of a direct sales approach either during or after the call.

3. Companies should accept responsibility for statements made by their sales staff or agents.

Reasonable Hours

1. Telephone marketers should avoid making sales and marketing calls during hours which are unreasonable to the recipients of the calls, bearing in mind that the OFT recommends that calls to consumers should not be made later than 9.00 pm unless expressly invited and that what is regarded as unreasonable can vary in different parts of the country and in different types of households or businesses.

2. When sales and marketing calls are initiated by a company or its representatives, telephone marketers should ask whether the timing of a call is convenient. If it is not, they should offer to ring back at a more convenient time.

Courtesy and Procedures

1. Normal rules of telephone courtesy should be observed. Telephone marketers should avoid the use of high pressure tactics which could be construed as harassment.

2. Telephone marketers should always recognise the right of the other party to terminate the telephone conversation at any stage, and should accept such termination promptly and courteously.

3. If, as a result of a telephone contact, an appointment is made whereby a representative of a company is to

visit a consumer at home, the consumer should be provided with a clearly identified contact point in order to facilitate possible cancellation or alteration of the appointment.

4. Confirmation of any order placed should be sent to the customer and any documents forwarded in accordance with the prevailing legislation.

5. Telephone marketers should take particular care not to seek information or to accept orders or appointments or invite any other action from a minor.

6. When consumer sales and marketing calls are made by a company or its representatives, there should be a cooling off period of at least 7 days for oral contracts resulting from such calls, and the recipients of the calls should be so informed.

Restriction of Contacts

1. Sales and Marketing calls should not be generated by random or sequential dialling manually or by computer.

2. Sales and Marketing calls should not knowingly be made to unlisted or ex-directory numbers.

3. Unless expressly invited consumer calls should not be made to individuals at their place of work.

4. Members should subscribe to the Telephone Preference Service (when it becomes available).

5. Members should delete from their telephone contact lists those persons who have specifically requested not to be contacted by telephone for sales or marketing purposes.

6. When sales and marketing calls are initiated by a company or its repre-

sentatives and automatic message and recording equipment is used, it is necessary either to:

a. Immediately effect an introduction on the lines of 'This is a computer call on behalf of . . .'

or

b. Have a 'Live' operator introduce the call under those circumstances where the nature of the call is of a personal or a sensitive nature.

Definitions

1. **Business calling**: Sales and Marketing calls, for an individual as a representative of his or her company.

2. **Consumer calling**: Sales and Marketing calls for an individual not as a representative of his or her employer or company.

3. **Sales & Marketing call**: A call designed to generate a sale of a product or service, or to lead toward a sale of a product or service to the specific company or consumer as a result of the information given during a telephone conversation.

Personnel

Insist on meeting the key people who would be handling your promotion: the telephone sales manager, supervisor and, where possible, the team. Judge the company by their interest and enthusiasm towards your project. If the communicators are critical of the success of your telephone marketing campaign, ask: What is their background? How much training have they received from the bureau? Are they rewarded adequately? If the bureau tell you that none of this is your business, make sure you don't give them your business!

Quality control

Look carefully into methods of quality control. Will you be

expected to brief supervisor and communicators yourself? If the answer is 'yes' this is another plus point.

Ask to see records currently kept, and check out reporting systems. If the system is computerized, make sure that there are adequate back-up facilities and any manual records are carefully maintained. Visit the offices. If the communicators are noisy without being loud, sell without harassing the prospects and the supervisor is on the spot listening to calls, then it is very likely you have found a professional telephone marketing bureau which will assist in providing you with a profitable promotion.

The bottom line

How much should you pay and on what basis? There is no set pattern at the moment in the charges made by the different bureaux. Some charge by the hour. They will make the maximum number of calls for you during that period, and an initial test run should tell you exactly what to expect in terms of cost per sale, or per contact.

A setting up charge is usual. This will probably cover the briefing session, devising and printing and alterations to the script and any specific recording procedure necessary for your particular project.

Some bureaux charge per call, or by contact, or even by completed script. The first can be quite expensive as it may take several calls before an actual contact is made. Hourly rates often include British Telecom meter unit charges: other companies charge these out separately, either at cost or plus a small percentage.

All these factors need to be carefully checked, so that 'hidden charges' don't appear upon completion of the campaign, throwing the economics of the exercise into confusion.

Even with your own in-house department it's worth considering a bureau

Consumer calling is usually most effective after business hours and at weekends. It is often uneconomical to keep offices open at these times, and a bureau can be the answer in situations like this, as well as at times of overloading.

The criteria for employing a bureau must be 'when outside is either cheaper, better or more available than inside'. As a parallel, many companies with vast computer mainframe installations find it more efficient to use outside agencies in maintaining their direct mail files.

Fine tuning of your own department may well indicate that there are certain areas which could be cost-effectively subcontracted to a bureau, releasing your own department for more involved projects requiring detailed knowledge of the product or service being sold. Functions such as reactivating lapsed accounts and updating mailing lists would probably be more efficient and cost-effective if undertaken by an outside agency, while the in-house team is used to obtain orders and upsell to current customers.

Once you have established a good relationship with a bureau and they develop an awareness of your product or service, it is then possible to delegate specific work as the need arises with the minimum time loss or disruption of schedules.

4

Setting up an in-house telephone marketing department

We'll make do now and if it works we'll spend some money and set it up properly.

Whoa. Stop right there. It is *not* a question of taking a telephone, a clerk with some time to spare and a desk – and using this as a test operation. You need to know facts and figures which can only be obtained by running a full-time team dedicated totally to the project. So, apart from immediately expending £X thousand in setting-up an operation 'blind', how do you find out exactly what you can expect to achieve – in fact, the economics of the situation?

Test first of all

The answer is at hand. Having decided on the functions of your proposed department, the prudent marketing manager will give a brief to two reputable outside bureaux and ask each to conduct a test campaign of at least 1,000 calls on its behalf. If the objective is to use the telephone for more than one purpose, it would be wise to have a test conducted on each, as a separate issue. For example, you may wish to:

- Reactivate lapsed accounts
- Service low-volume business
- Produce qualified sales leads
- Sell your product directly
- Find new prospects
- Undertake research

Brief the bureau exactly as you would your own salespeople, and make it quite clear to each agency that you will want detailed information upon completion of the test.

Provide literature and point-of-sale material. Discuss your objectives fully and at length. Insist on meeting and talking with the communicators and supervisors who will be working on your project. Ask if you may visit the bureau while the campaign is taking place, and do so more than once if you can. A good agency will counsel you in depth, determining the position of telephone marketing in your media mix and working out with you an effective script and method of approach. Don't crowd the agency. Be content to let them formulate and test out various proposals so that you gain the full benefit of their experience. After all there is little point in paying for advice if you don't take it.

If you divide the test between two bureaux, it is essential that all the basic input provided to them is geographically the same.

Give each a section covering similar demographics, and time the operation so that it takes place concurrently.

When the tests are completed, the analysis supplied by each bureau should provide you with the answer to the question: 'Will telephone marketing work for my company?'

Take the average of the information supplied unless there is a large discrepancy between the two figures in which case the test should be extended to a third outside source. As a general rule a difference of up to 20 per cent between the results of two agencies is quite acceptable.

Data needed from the test

1   Average number of diallings per hour per person
2   Average number of contacts made per person
3   Average number of meter units per contact – ask for two figures here – standard and peak rate calling
4   Actual number of diallings and total meter units overall
5   Positive responses
6   Number of those interested
7   Negatives
8   Detailed reasons for refusals
9   The 'nixies' (unobtainable or moved away) on your list
10 The most frequent objections received

Ask each of the bureaux for a 'roll-on' price per contact if they were to run the operation for you on a long-term basis. The information you received could look like this:

Report on telephone marketing test of 1,000 contacts to client's list of lapsed customers

Duration of test	98 hours
Number of communicators	3
Total diallings	1440
Total contacts	989
Positive responses	137
Require further information	222
Negative	540
Need to be called back	46
Unobtainable	90
Total British Telecom (meter) Units	7250

Reasons for negative responses (individually shown on scripts in detail)

48% dissatisfied with service;
21% obtained better price from main competitor;
29% X Company rep visited more frequently and order placed with him
2% unwilling to comment

Using the average figure obtained by combining the totals of the two bureaux, you will then be able to judge whether the cost of setting up an in-house division is likely to be justified by the results achieved.

Costs of the department per annum (£)

3 telephone rentals	1,521.00
BTU	13,000.00
Communicator's salary (×3)	33,000.00
Supervisor	13,500.00
Printing, clerk, computer time	12,500.00
Overheads and canteen	6,500.00
Setting up & briefing	3,000.00
Scriptwriting & re-writes	4,000.00
Accounting, executive input	8,000.00
	£95,021.00

With three communicators expected to make, say, 80 successful sales calls per week, the average cost to the company would be:

80 successful contacts × 3 communicators × 50 weeks p.a. = 12,000 successful calls
Cost per positive call = 7.91

However, most of the overhead costs would remain static for a larger number of communicators and the cost per sales call would be reduced accordingly. Compare your own costs to the 'roll on' figure quoted by the more successful bureau. If both are equal, and the cost per successful contact is profitable within your own financial structuring, you are on the right track and ready to begin setting up your department.

Setting up the department

Remember though that it is difficult to make a cake without breaking eggs. Referring back to the beginning of this chapter, don't fall into the trap of trying to 'make do' by using existing staff with time to spare. Consider these *don'ts*.

Don't employ people your personnel department are trying to 'offload'.
Don't employ the MD's niece who wants something to do.
Don't even think about the not-so-good salesman who wants 'a change' from being on the road.

Start at the very beginning. Where is the department going to be located? A bright room with natural light is essential. Invest in a thick pile carpet, and ensure that the walls and ceiling are soundproofed as much as possible.

Cork is an ideal top material for the walls. As well as providing additional soundproofing, it will allow for point-of-sale materials, notices and other information to be easily affixed.

Good ventilation and heating are particularly important in a telephone sales department, as well as easy access to a canteen for drinks and smoking. In our firm we allow a twenty-minute 'break' in every three-hour session. This can be taken in one, or offered as two breaks of ten minutes each. Somewhere to hang outdoor clothes and lockers must be provided, and communicators should be discouraged from bringing newspapers and any other bric-à-brac into the room.

Rules are necessary and should be simple but firmly maintained. For example, in our firm we stipulate:

1 Hours of working
2 Canteen break details
3 No smoking
4 Outdoor clothing to be put in lockers and no items other than handbags allowed in the room
5 Drinks and food to be consumed in canteen only
6 Punctuality essential
7 Method and time of payment
8 The in-house telephone number to be given out to those prospects wishing to call back
9 Conditions of employment

An easel and board is an important piece of equipment and forms the focus of the room. Information on each particular project, individual results and incentives should all be displayed on the board.

The names of the communicators should be written-up daily with their successful results immediately marked-up either by the supervisor as they are achieved or by the communicators themselves. Either way this provides excellent motivation for the communicators. We all like to be seen to do as well, if not better than, our neighbour, and will strive harder if our results are not as good.

Don't install desks. These encourage unnecessary clutter and mess. Plain 6 ft × 4 ft tables are sufficient, with triple filing baskets on each one to hold the paperwork. Depending on the number of people in the room, the tables need not be separated. Where there are eight or more communicators, the ideal grouping is in lots of four. This encourages motivation through propinquity: and a good supervisor will make sure that there is a more successful communicator acting as pace-setter in each group.

Chairs should be comfortable, with good back support and

without arms. We find that cloth coverings are better than vinyl which can get sticky in warmer weather.

Plenty of shelves are needed for telephone and other directories and the books should be meticulously maintained in alphabetical order. It is possible to place a permanent order with British Telecom for new issues of the telephone books as they are published.

As the bulletin board is the focal point of the room, all of the communicators should be faced accordingly: and a desk should be placed at the side of the board for the supervisor.

How many chiefs and how many Indians?

A department of four people does not justify more than one manager to supervise, maintain records and produce the daily analysis. Employ more than this number of communicators and you will need to have both a manager and a supervisor on the team. If the sole function of the department is to contact existing customers and your list is readily available together with telephone numbers, the manager will be responsible for making sure that there are sufficient contact forms available for each day's calling. Where the intention is to open up new prospect files, it may very well be that you will need to employ a clerk to research new names and addresses and verify telephone numbers. The latter is a laborious and time-consuming job which should not be given to the communicators – whose function is to talk to as many of your prospects as possible within a working day.

Job functions

The Manager

WANTED

Sales Manager, Public Relations Officer,
Personnel Manager, Administrator,
Analyst

The successful telephone sales manager needs to be able to combine all of these jobs. He must be capable of administrating a department competently, hiring and firing fairly, motivating enthusiastically, producing analysis accurately and providing management with projections promptly and with foresight.

There aren't many trained people around already skilled in these attributes who have previous experience as a telephone sales manager. The industry is too new. If you are unable to head-hunt, I suggest you look at two other possibilities.

1 Consider interviewing assistant sales managers, or very experienced field representatives, who have successfully worked and been trained by thorough organizations such as IBM. An enthusiasm to get into telephone marketing management, coupled with a good sales background, can result in first-rate administrators. Check carefully into previous involvement with records and give a plus point where the applicant has some knowledge of computer techniques.
2 You will almost certainly receive applications from tele-phone communicators who think they would make good managers. Don't dismiss them lightly. Contact the previous employer to check on success rates, punctuality, accuracy in filling out records and ability to get on well with other members of the team.

Supervisor

Although it is easier to fill the position of supervisor than it is to hire a manager, the supervisor should have the ability to maintain existing procedures, yet be flexible enough to alter requirements as needs arise. An important element of the job is to communicate with the operators so that the specific objective of each campaign is clearly understood.

The supervisor should be capable of running the training and re-training programmes and be completely *au fait* with the scripts, objections and answers, as well as having an accurate understanding of the number of diallings which could reasonably be expected to be made by each communicator.

'Warning bells' should ring in the mind of a good supervisor as soon as there is a lessening in the number of diallings made or results are not as good as previously. Steps should be quickly taken to re-motivate, improve scripts or re-train.

The supervisor should have first-hand knowledge of having worked as a telephone communicator, and because of this it is often possible to promote from an existing team.

Communicators

What kind of staff should I employ? Full or part-time? There are two schools of thought here. Personally I find that part-time personnel make better communicators. Working a three-hour shift only, with a 20-minute break, under a competent supervisor, it is easier to sustain the necessary three E's which make a vital and satisfactory department:

> **Enthusiasm**
> **Energy**
> **Effectiveness**

Part-time people may be housewives, students, actors ('resting' members of the acting profession make first-rate communicators) or anybody else wishing to work three hours a day, such as single parents. An interesting part-time job is not easy to obtain, and I find that staff employed on this basis are more anxious to work and keep their job than many full-time employees, although there is considerably more movement in 'coming and going' and length of employment tends to be for shorter periods than with full-time staff. On the other hand, full-time staff have a greater tendency to develop company loyalty and are generally more committed to the job.

In Chapter 2 I had the drastic sub-heading 'Improve or remove'. This really upset a telephone marketing consultant asked to give an opinion on this book. He implied that my attitude was too tough in this report. Believe me, anybody who runs a successful department will tell you that it pays to 'fire' poor communicators sooner rather than later. Unless there is an obvious improvement in the approach and achievements of a particular operator, it is essential to dismiss the offender quickly for the well-being of the whole unit. Good telephone communicators are competitive people who will try and improve on the results achieved by their neighbour. One person consistently producing lower results can easily de-motivate and lower the average throughout the department. The 'wait and see' manager who is hesitant to terminate through kindness (or lethargy) often lives to regret his action.

Be fair though. Make the position quite clear at commencement of employment. Explain the average diallings currently achieved, and the expected results. Speak plainly about the company's policy of hiring and firing, and the reasons why it is not possible to stay with failure. My company monitors each communicator for two days after training is completed; if after this period of time the results are not within 50 per cent of minimum expectations, we immediately dispense with the operator's services.

Recruitment

If you decide to employ full-time communicators the usual avenues of newspaper advertisements etc. are the best place to look. For part-time staff try *The Stage*, local employment offices and university personnel officers. My company has had many excellent communicators who have worked on a part-time basis for three or four years while they have been at college.

The first and main interview should be by telephone. The form illustrated in Figure 4 has been deliberately designed to encourage the impatient candidate who has insufficient patience to be a communicator to show visibly his irritation at the inanities and format of the questions asked. If the candidate comes over well at this first interview, there should be a 90 per cent possibility that you have a good communicator in the making. Forget about everything else when you finally come face-to-face for the second interview. One of the best communicators my company ever had was an elderly lady who wore white gloves and a picture hat throughout the day, and consistently turned in high verified sales results. Another young man wore different coloured wellington boots every day and his waist-length hair was tucked into a cummerband. He was our most successful communicator for a whole year. Had these interviews

Figure 4 Interview form

PAULINE MARKS TELEPHONE INTERVIEW FORM

INTERVIEW TIME
IF SET AFTER THIS   Date:
TELEPHONE
INTERVIEW   Time:

"I'm sure you have some questions about the job, but first let me ask you some questions about yourself."

How did you hear about the job? _____

		Today's Date _____
1. Name _____	Phone _____	
2. Address _____	How long at this address?	+( ) over six months −( ) less than six months
"We're at _____	How far is that from you? Travelling time from us?	+( ) less than 20 minutes −( ) more than 20 minutes
3. Last job _____	How long were you employed?	+( ) more than 1 year −( ) less than 1 year
	Pay at last job?	+( ) more than £7,500 p.a. (£150 per week) −( ) less
	How many employers in last 5 years?	+( ) less than 3 −( ) more than 3
4. Job Skills	Can you write clearly?	+( ) yes −( ) no
	Do you like to talk on phone?	+( ) yes

Have you ever sold anything?   – ( ) no
                                                      + ( ) yes

INTERVIEWER
Rate quality of phone voice.   – ( ) no
                                                      + ( ) very good
                                                      – ( ) less than very good

5. Total – ( ) from above _____. If more than 3. say "Thank you for your interest in the job, but we have had others apply that have had more of
the experience we are looking for."

If less than 3, say "I have just a couple more questions I'd like to ask before we set up an interview for you."

6. Are you looking for part time work?   ( ) Yes   ( ) No

7. The starting pay is _____ per hour. Would that be acceptable to you?   ( ) Yes   ( ) No

8. The job mainly involves communicating with business people over the telephone at their place of
business. We have an excellent training programme. Does this sound like something you might be
interested in?   ( ) Yes   ( ) No

9. If the answer to Nos. 6, 7 & 8 is yes, say, "It sounds like we should discuss the job further. Could you come in at
_____ for a personal interview with _____?

He will answer any questions you might have at that time.

been face-to-face rather than by phone, there is no way at all that either of these people would have been employed in the bureau.

Sometimes, particularly when showing visitors around the department, I feel that we are operating with ex-employees of the Barnum and Bailey Circus – yet if we shut our eyes and listen to the enthusiastic and melodious voices, I wonder instead whether we may be employing ex-members of the Royal Shakespeare Company.

Records

Once you have employed the communicators, and immediately embarked on a carefully planned and controlled training programme, it is essential that you have clear recording procedures before the operation actually starts.

Records are particularly important in a telephone marketing department. They immediately indicate weak spots and, read carefully, will foretell impending problems. They take the guesswork (and possible bias) out of management, and are totally essential to the success of the whole campaign. Without an effective recording system it is difficult to maintain growth and make the best possible use of available resources.

The best record system must be one which is simple for the communicators to maintain, and easy for management to analyze and use to improve performance. The information obtained should increase profitability by clearly pinpointing areas in which results are falling behind the general trend and enable management to rectify the trouble. It is only through good recording that it is possible not only to improve a situation, but, even more importantly, to obtain a clear understanding of what the problem actually is.

There are always 'high flyers' in every telephone marketing department, and the differential between their results and 'Mr Average' can be as high as a 2:1 ratio. In a well-managed office the 'high flyer' is carefully used as a pacesetter while at the same time every effort is made to see that the extraordinary results are used to motivate rather than to discourage the average operator.

Most successful departments run on an hourly basis and the communicator's call record card could look like the one shown in Figure 5.

Figure 5 Communicator's daily call report

Communicator _____ Ref _____
Date _____

Hours	Diallings	Contacts	Positives	F/I	N/I	N/R	N/E
1	25	10	3	4	2	1	–
2	26	9	3	2	1	2	1
3	20	8	1	2	1	4	–
4	26	11	4	–	3	4	–
5	25	10	3	2	–	5	–
6	22	8	1	1	1	5	–
TOTAL	144	56	15	11	8	21	1

Note
F/I – Further Information required
N/I – Not Interested
N/R – No Reply
N/E – Non-existent

Analyzing results

Presuming that the operator is working from 10 am to 5 pm with a one-hour lunch break between 1 pm and 2 pm, it becomes obvious to management that the third and last hours of the day need re-vitalizing. Fewer diallings have been made with the result that there are fewer positive responses. The answer here is to motivate by incentives during these periods. My company usually offers a cash payment for the most positive responses, together with a different incentive for the largest number of diallings made. This gives an opportunity for both the high flyer and Mr Average to exceed their previous totals and re-motivates the whole department.

The other message immediately apparent from the record card in Figure 5 is that more prospects are unavailable in the afternoon for this particular project. The answer here ideally is to eliminate the afternoon session and double up the staff for the morning period when more prospects would appear to be available. This is not always practical in an in-house situation, and the solution could be to extend working hours to test response from an evening or weekend session.

It can happen quite legitimately that a communicator will

42

Figure 6 Weekly management call record card

Date _____ Comments _____

	Diallings	Contacts	Pos	F/I	N/I	N/R	N/E	Total hours worked	BTU
1									
2									
3									
4									
5									
6									
Total									

work for a three-hour session and not achieve any positive results. It can happen, but it is very rare and should not go unchecked. It is not unknown for an operator to falsify the number of diallings made, but use of call-log or similar computer equipment will verify each report as well as provide the number of BTU. Automatic Switching Ltd, Mitcham, Surrey supply Audiotext with equipment which provides continuos 'on demand' managers' reports and a continuos cost summary (Figure 7). If the reason is not through tardiness in making too few diallings, the trouble must lay with the method of presenting. In any event accurate and frequent reading of the records will enable management to rectify the problems.

Figure 7 On demand manager's report: Deparment cost summary

TNA25 Department cost summary Dated Fri 06/Dec/85 to Thu 19/Dec/85
Department 2 Sales 2

	Local		STD		IDO		Total	
Line	Calls	Cost	Calls	Cost	Calls	Cost	Calls	Cost
1223	18	1.01	33	18.26	0	.00	51	19.27
1224	14	1.41	9	2.20	0	.00	23	3.61
1225	13	1.01	11	3.21	0	.00	24	4.22
1226	13	.62	6	1.01	0	.00	19	1.63
1227	15	1.10	6	.88	0	.00	21	1.98
1228	128	7.66	17	4.71	0	.00	145	12.37
1229	21	1.45	5	1.41	0	.00	26	2.86
1230	1	.04	8	.75	7	2.11	16	2.90
1231	5	.70	9	4.36	0	.00	14	5.06
1232	8	.44	1	.22	0	.00	9	.66
	236	15.44	105	37.00	7	2.11	348	54.56

BENEFITS:
* Affords departmental cost allocation, encouraging managerial responsibility and accountability.
* Provides analysis for individual managers and devolves responsibility for constraining costs.
* Allows departmental budgets to be set.
* Highlights unusually high expenditure.
* Used to check against telephone bill.

Figure 8 Weekly management sales leads report

Date _____ Comments _____

Total leads issued this week:

Cumulative total of leads:

Advised as contacted:

Outstanding to be contacted:

Salesman	Leads this week	Cumulative	Contacted	To contact
A				
B				
C				
D				
E				
F				
G				
H				

One card cannot be taken in isolation. Totalling all the records on an hourly basis will produce average figures for each period, and at the same time indicate those communicators producing less effective returns. BTU (meter units) should also be evaluated against each individual's results. This could show that some communicators are holding lengthy conversations without results – or the reverse could also be true.

The individual records should be entered onto a master sheet, which again should be as simple as circumstances allow (see Figure 6).

It may be that you are using the telephone marketing department to obtain leads for salesmen or for research such as product, price, seasonal or demographic testing. Perhaps you intend to sell directly. All of these functions need separate call reporting; and the emphasis should always be to produce the least complicated sheet necessary, coupled with an effective filing system. Salesmen's leads need particular attention and the weekly management report (see Figure 8) should show the exact position encompassing both the figures produced by the communicators and the follow-up by the salesforce.

I always recall with horror the 150 timed and verified appointments within one month made throughout the Greater London area for one company. The job was undertaken through their agency who 'forgot' to let us know that the client's salesforce was reduced to just two. The result was that 100 expensively acquired 'leads' were totally ignored. With a weekly information report in front of management, danger signals can quickly be read, not only by the sales manager, but also by the telephone manager who can either increase the operation as necessary, or reduce the number of leads being obtained *pro tem* until the field force catches up.

If the telephone manager and the sales manager are one and the same, there is no difficulty in obtaining this information – but in a larger organization problems of communication do occur (and in not-so-large companies too). It's worth inviting everyone's cooperation at the outset. Point out the truth of the matter. *Everyone*, including the individual salesperson, benefits from clear accurate records.

5

Overcoming objections

'What is in it for me?'
'What's the catch?'
'I really don't need it . . .'
'Can't afford it at the moment . . .'
'I'll think about it'
'I have to ask the boss/wife/colleague'
'I've managed without one so far'
'Call me next week'
'I've never heard of your company'

Many people object to the EEC, some can't stand Margaret Thatcher, some detest the colour of your carpet, the car you're driving, the package holiday you choose, and probably even the colour of your underpants if they knew it. So, don't be surprised if they object to your telephone solicitation. It is, after all, totally in character.

You don't have to be a 'professional objector' of course to say 'no' automatically to a telephone (or indeed any other) sales presentation. The communicator's skill comes in defining the true reason for the objection.

There are really five possible objections to any sales pitch.

'I can't afford it' (Lack of money)
'I'm not in a hurry' (I can always order at a later date)
'I have no need' (What will I do with it?)
'Not interested' (Lack of confidence)
'It's just rubbish' (Don't understand what is being sold)

A good sales presentation is designed to draw a few 'yes's' from the prospect. This is done to make it easier for him or her to say 'yes' at the time it counts most. Never consider the possibilities of asking someone if they are interested. This is always sudden death! You put the prospect on the spot with this approach by

46

giving him a choice of 'yes' or 'no', something or nothing. Always ensure presenters offer a choice of something and something. Put the pressure on the product rather than the prospect. Instead of 'Would you like to buy Buckingham Palace, Mrs Smith?' the correct approach is 'Would you prefer Buckingham Palace or Hampton Court, Mrs Smith?'

Bearing in mind that the prospect will not particularly wish to be sold, he will certainly appreciate an opportunity of making a choice. Beware, though, not to give too many choices: this can be self-defeating.

If a customer tells you he won't see the rep this time round, he is waivering. The benefits should be used as an inducement, possibly emphasizing the limited availability or keenness of the price structure – and endeavouring to get across the message that any delay could be giving up a golden opportunity. The main negative reasons or objections should be known immediately, as a result of an initial test of the telephone campaign, combined with knowledge obtained from the company's records and salesforce. These should form part of the original briefing to the communicators, and they should always be provided with a list to which they can refer.

The simplest method is to mount some small plastic envelopes measuring around 16 × 11cm onto a cardboard approximately 27cm square. The end-result will be an easily accessible flip-up chart which will assist the communicators to sell the benefits of the programme and reinforce their memory in emphasizing the key points of the promotion.

If the prospect objects to the proposal, probe the true reason and refer to the appropriate response. Consider the following:

Can't afford
I'll think about it
Don't really need it
I have to ask the wife/husband
Thinking about it
Call back next week
Competition is better

The objections voiced by the prospect are not always the true reasons for saying 'no'. People do not always say what they mean – or indeed mean what they say.

The communicator must probe as skilfully as possible, seeking clues to the true reasons for the negative reaction to the proposal, by encouraging the prospect to talk and discuss the offer in greater detail. The right questions carefully structured beforehand, and continued (but not extensive) dialogue will usually indicate the exact reasons for the refusal.

'Don't really need it' could mean that the benefits have not been clearly understood, and the communicator should re-emphasize the value of these. Alternatively the prospect may really be saying that it is too expensive for his current budget. The answer to this problem should be conveyed as an additional benefit, particularly if there is a form of easy-payment scheme available.

'Thinking about it' or 'Call back next week' could just be a polite way of saying that the prospect is not interested. The communicator should treat this type of response as an opportunity of reinforcing the sales pitch by answering with 'Yes, but . . .' and repeating the benefits.

Probing and overcoming negative responses

It is more than likely that the reason for the initial lack of enthusiasm is because of the communicator not convincing the prospect that he should take the decision to buy now.

If there is an exceptional benefit to offer, the telephone marketer should not be afraid of repetition, and should interject answers to any interruption during the presentation.

An important and essential way of overcoming objections is by having confidence in the product or service being sold. It is a rewarding experience to listen to someone who radiates confidence. He or she sounds sincere, attentive and interesting. The person believes in his product, believes in his company and believes in himself. The prospect will rely on his judgment, trust him, want to buy from him. Communicators must have a positive and enthusiastic attitude in order to convince those who are reluctant to buy. Above all they must not fear explaining the costs involved in purchasing the product they are trying to sell –but rather emphasize its worth to the prospective customers.

'I have to ask my boss/husband/wife' should be pursued by the communicator with 'Yes, but you do agree that the XYZ wordprocessor is just what you need, don't you, Miss Brown?'

If Miss Brown agrees, the next stage is to try and get her consent to make a reservation subject to approval of the third party.

'With your permission, I will reserve an XYZ processor for seven days at the special rate for you. If your boss doesn't agree that an XYZ will not only make work more pleasant for you but also produce professional letters to a very high standard, we will of course cancel the reservation immediately. If this is acceptable, I will call back in seven days and you can let me know his decision.'

The same objection could also mean that Miss Brown was not the correct decision-maker to contact, and tactful questioning should lead to the name of the person responsible for purchasing new equipment.

'I've managed without one so far' Yes, but . . . his competitors haven't and they are doubtless highly delighted with the additional business it brings them.

Mrs Brown may still be taking her washing to the launderette, and explains that at £2.00 a week, she can use the service for five years for the cost of the washing machine the telephone marketer is trying to sell to her. Yes, Mrs Brown, but . . .

'Consider the inconvenience when the weather is bad, or wasting summer evenings and weekends sitting in the hot, stuffy launderette.'

'Of course a machine in your own home means that the only washing which goes into it is your own and your family's.'

'A washing machine is so much whiter, more hygienic and readily available.'

'Once it is paid for, the cost is nil. We operate an excellent service maintenance contract, and the average life of one machine is 12 years.'

'A washing machine in your own home is almost a status symbol. There are X per cent households with them in your TV area.'

Talking the points through and encouraging dialogue will 'prod' the prospect into revealing the true objections and give the communicator every opportunity to reply with the pre-determined responses.

When does selling turn into harassment?

If the lady is 87, she won't want to buy life insurance! The border line between hard-selling and trying hard to sell is a very narrow one, and communicators must be taught the importance of not stepping into the dangerous area of 'pushing' a sale too much. Not only may such action actively damage the seller's image, it can also result in a disproportionately high level of refusal to accept goods, and subsequent denials of agreements made on the telephone.

Benjamin Franklin said 'Lose no time. Be always employed in something useful. Cut off all unnecessary actions.' Once a sale is made congratulations are in order. This is a success story, but being a good loser is part of the selling game, and if a negative response is still received after all benefits have been repeatedly stated, and there is no indication that the prospect may change his mind, it makes good sense to close the call quickly and courteously and to start again as soon as possible with the next person on the list. Time wasted is money down the drain. Always remember that telephone marketing is a numbers game – the more calls made, the higher the number of orders received. There are no success rules that will work unless this is always borne in mind.

What does OFTEL have to say about telephone selling?

OFTEL (the British Telecom 'watchdog') has been vigilant in looking at telephone selling, and has consistently undertaken surveys in order to judge whether the guidelines laid down by the telephone committee of the British Direct Marketing Association have been efficacious in controlling the consumer calling which seems to worry Director General Bryan Carsberg. In a report issued in December 1988, they stated that: 'In June 1988, two-thirds of those asked said they had received unsolicited telephone selling calls at home in the previous 12 months; the incidence of such calls is increasing. The respondent had usually had no previous contact with the firm, which most commonly was selling double glazing or fitted kitchens. In a significant minority of cases, the caller did not initially make clear that it was a sales call. A large majority of respondents objected to sales calls and wanted action taken to curtail them. I regard forcing selling calls on unwilling recipients as diminishing quality of service and I intend to keep the development of this phenomenon under review.'

You will note that Prof. Carsberg refers to selling by telephone as a 'phenomenon' – but the 'complaints' received seem to be basically about a very limited area of the industry, and should not be confused with responsible telephone marketing which I believe accounts for the vast majority of calls made.

The same report from OFTEL in a paragraph headed 'Telephone Selling' states that:

No comments were made in this Report on Business Telephone Marketing, and I would add that in the decade since our PHONESELL division started to make outbound calls, we have recorded no more than two handfuls of adverse criticism from prospects.

We do not therefore believe that the comments are indicative of the public's opinion as a whole. After all, nobody complains about the fact that the newspapers, magazines, radio and TV all take up time and space with advertising products which may or may not be known to us. The option is always there to put down a phone if the subscriber doesn't wish to talk. Conversely, many people welcome the opportunity of talking personally to an expert, giving them the chance to ask questions without being forced into a commitment, which can occur if the meeting had taken place face to face.

Telephone selling

A survey conducted by the National Opinion Poll for OFTEL in June (of 1,853 people aged 15 or over) asked respondents about their experience of and attitude towards the use of the telephone for sales approaches to individual consumers. Two-thirds of respondents with a telephone reported having received unsolicited telephone selling calls at home in the previous 12 months. Statistical studies have demonstrated a tendency for respondents to misjudge – to shorten – timescales when responding to questions involving the recall of past events. Some of the calls reported can be assumed to have occurred more than a year previously and therefore some of those (20 per cent of respondents) reporting only one or two calls may not have experienced any such calls in the 12-month period.

Subscribers receiving telephone selling calls at home in previous 12 months

Date of Survey	Percentage who received calls*
September 1985	46
September 1986	48
September 1987	54
June 1988	67

Note: * Thought to be a slight overestimate (see text).
Source: NOP (Market Research) Ltd

Comparison with the results of earlier surveys shows that the incidence of telephone selling calls has increased.

The tendency of respondents to shorten timescales and include calls received more than a year previously has a much more serious effect on estimates of the numbers of subscribers receiving calls. Although the average number of calls claimed by those with a telephone at home was seven in the June 1988 survey, the true level is probably about five calls a year.

Double glazing and fitted kitchens feature prominently in the list of products and services offered by telephone sellers.

Nearly 80 per cent of those receiving calls said that the calls were made mainly in the evening or at weekends. Around 90 per cent said that they had no previous contacts with any of the firms making the calls; this is probably an overestimate through failure to remember a contact, or because a contact which prompted the call had been with another member of the family. Around 95 per cent of those receiving calls say that they never respond positively.

It was difficult to obtain information about the way the sales call was conducted because many respondents had experienced several calls and hence a range of approaches. Nevertheless, it was found that in a large majority of calls the salesperson set out the purpose of the call at the start and provided the name of his/her company. On the other hand, a third of respondents had experienced calls where they were not aware until a late stage that it was a sales call, and the pretence of conducting research was used in a significant proportion of such calls. Around ten per cent of those respondents who had asked callers for the name of their company had encountered at least one refusal to give the name. Among respondents who had asked a caller where he/she had obtained the telephone number, around 20 per cent had encountered at least one refusal to say.

Respondents reporting telephone selling calls, by type of product or service

Type of product or service	Percentages	
	of those receiving calls	of those with telephone
Life insurance	10	6
Other insurance	7	4
Financial advice	7	5
Double glazing/window replacement	77	50
Loft insulation	4	2
Central heating	4	2
Showers	2	1
Fitted kitchen	50	33
Other general building services	6	4
Home security systems	3	2
Books/magazine	2	1
Carpet cleaning	3	2
Other*	21	14
Can't remember	4	2

Note: * Known to include some which might have been regarded as building services.
Source: NOP (Market Research) Ltd.

What should be done about sales calls?

| | **Percentages** | |
Action	of those receiving calls	of those with telephone
Should be banned by law	32	30
Should be some control	50	49
Nothing needs to be done	15	15
No opinion/don't know	3	6
	100	100
Should be avoidable without going ex-directory	81	79

Source: NOP (Market Research) Ltd

Nearly three-quarters of respondents who had sales calls in the previous 12 months objected to receiving calls. Even among those who had not had calls recently, most objected. Reflecting the strength of feeling against sales calls, the table above shows that around 80 per cent of respondents thought that action should be taken.

6

Using incentives to motivate

Advertisements similar to the above appear in abundance every day in the classified advertising sections of the newspapers. The job description sounds glamorous; but before you know it in front of you is a script and a pile of telephone numbers. You now face the prospect of spending the next few hours dialling, repeating the same message, concluding your 'spiel' and then starting all over again.

Frankly the work is tedious. You don't see the face of the person to whom you are talking, and unless some interest in the form of an incentive is introduced, the boredom you feel is reflected in your voice to the detriment of the success of the telephone calls being made.

In order to overcome this problem it is necessary for managers to implement means of motivation by developing strategies which will interest the communicators and encourage them to treat each prospect as an individual call rather than as just one of the day's production line.

Salary vs commission

It is very advantageous to the manager in those situations where a firm cost-per-hour is negotiated to pay a definite salary to the communicators. It also enables the supervisor to ensure a certain level of output and most importantly it negates the aggressive 'hard' sell which can actively damage a campaign if the situation is allowed to get out of hand. An effective communicator being paid per order or for each appointment achieved will usually produce better results than if paid at an hourly rate. When analyzing the final results, however, it is often found that orders acquired by aggressive telephone selling are frequently cancelled and appointments made in this way often do not end in sales – possibly because the prospects feel that they have been forced into a situation against their own judgment. The communicator may also be tempted to create leads with unqualified prospects.

Conversely, while personnel are generally happier to have the assurance of a guaranteed level of income, it also means that, generally speaking, they will not make the effort to reach higher levels of productivity. This lack of effort can lead in turn to mediocrity and a lowering of standards.

Incentives

Good morning communicators. These are your calls for today. I expect at least 20 diallings every hour. Good luck. Get to it!

After committing so much money and time to hiring and training the right people for your job, it is foolish not to spend thought on motivating to avoid constant turnover and employee burn-out. A manager needs to devote considerable time to thinking of incentives which will motivate, and help to create an environment that makes expectations very clear in order to provide the feedback needed to improve attitudes.

There are some people who are motivated by pride alone in achieving good results. For most, however, this is not enough. They need to be recognized as human beings not as robots, and respond to award and compensatory schemes for their efforts. Money is, of course, the main motivator, although not necessarily so, and the ideal incentive scheme should be a combination of both.

My company's telephone marketing manager discovered that in the sixth hour of making commercial sales calls (between 4 and 5 pm) we were achieving a lower rate of diallings – and, subsequently, a lower number of contacts and sales – than during the rest of the day. Enthusiasm had obviously flagged by the last period.

For five days, half the team were offered an incentive for the sixth hour. Comparative results for the same project showed:

	Hours 1–5 Average	Without incentive Hour 6 Average	With incentive Hour 6 Average
Diallings	364	298	370
Contacts	152	90	152
Sales	10	7	11

By using an incentive scheme, 24 per cent extra diallings resulted in a 69 per cent increase in contacts made and, not surprisingly, 57 per cent improvement in sales. Indeed, as in this instance, the sixth can often become the most productive hour of the working day.

The incentive need not necessarily be money. It can be a bottle of wine (a great favourite), an umbrella, sunglasses or a large box of chocolates, maybe even a theatre ticket. Often, in order to rekindle flagging enthusiasm, the supervisor makes a 'mystery' out of the incentive by writing the description on a piece of paper, folding it over and then pinning it to the board.

Salary plus bonus

Providing that the hourly payment is a reasonable one, the telephone manager can realistically hope to achieve and maintain a certain level of production by offering bonus payments for all contacts made above a minimum level.

If costings are worked out on the basis of paying the communicator, say, £5 per hour for an expected ten completed contacts, then by making a bonus payment of 50 pence for each contact in excess of this number the net effect is an incentive to increase production while maintaining cost per sale/enquiry.

This system needs detailed bookkeeping: but as long as the bonus does not exceed the hourly payment, it does not lead to 'hard' or aggressive selling.

Contests

There are many variations to the ways in which you can motivate a telephone marketing sales department. Pitting teams against each other brings out the competitive side of most people. Lunch for the winning team is a very acceptable reward, and pizzas and beer brought into the offices always bring 'crowing' noises from the winning team and encourage the unsuccessful communicators to 'beat' their colleagues the next day.

Individuals

Individual incentives can effectively be offered for

- Best results in a particular hour
- Most completed contacts in a working day
- Highest diallings in a period (needless to say more diallings lead to a greater amount of contacts and subsequently increased sales)

Lots of small incentives are more effective than large prizes. The latter, in any event, would nearly always be won by the same people each time. Every telephone marketing department has its 'high flyers'!

Lots of incentive prizes means that all the communicators will or should win something and this creates an excellent incentive for everybody to excel.

As an example, while selling a milk drink to 10,000 potential retail outlets, my company found that sales in the third and fourth day increased by 40 per cent. The satisfying result was due entirely to a very bright telephone supervisor who instituted a form of pass-the-parcel. This consisted of passing round a sealed envelope from communicator to communicator. They could only keep the envelope while they were actually talking to a prospect. The manager had pre-set an alarm clock, and, when the bell rang, whoever was holding the envelope was able to open it. Contents varied between £5, £10 and £15.

Number of diallings increased dramatically. Nobody wanted to miss out on a chance of holding the envelope. Perhaps the telephone supervisor was too good. He was subsequently head-hunted by our client!

General incentives

While it is wise materially to motivate in terms of immediate gain, there are also other ways of rewarding enthusiastic personnel. In-house promotion creates an upward mobility within a company which encourages the more ambitious communicators to strive for a higher level of production in order that they can be offered the same opportunities.

Obviously there can only be a few vacancies for supervisory and management jobs. However, a department can be run on two or more levels with payments adjusted *pro rata* to the level of work demanded. Therefore, the schedule should provide for the first level to undertake straightforward list research, customer service repeat calls, etc. and the second level of staffing being advanced to undertake more complex work with the communicators being rewarded accordingly. Promotion from one level to the next is excellent motivation and creates a competitive atmosphere which eliminates the lethargy which can otherwise creep in, with drastic results.

Participation

Successful scripts should always have been tested first of all before the roll out commences. The best way to test a script is to invite the participation of the communicators to criticize and suggest improvements based on their personal knowledge of the response achieved during the initial calls. Creating a team of involved people, who feel that they are an integral part of the company, contributing towards its success, is the very best motivation of all.

Ergonomics

In order to increase productivity, the good manager has to ensure successful interaction between his staff and the prospects at the end of the phone, by providing a good atmosphere in which the dialogues take place. Environment is particularly important.

Do ensure that physical requirements are met. The most complicated and advanced telecommunications equipment can fail if certain physical needs are not provided for.

Do provide motivational support at all times, varying it to coincide with the amount of additional effort needed for a particular function.

Do remember to recognize the individual needs of each communicator, and encourage them to personalize their work space. Photographs, small plants, etc. encourage them to identify and feel comfortable in their own space.

Do remember that lighting is particularly important, focusing on each work space.

A telephone marketing office buzzing with the noise of enthusiastic voices is one of the success signs I always look for; equally though one should not ignore the fact that peripheral equipment such as fax machines, photocopiers, wordprocessors, etc. can be a disruptive element. An investment in acoustic panels, thick carpeting and phones with lights instead of bells will cut down on the surrounding off-putting distractions.

Communicators need good chairs; comfortable with upright upholstered backs. A modern, ergonomically designed chair, will more than justify its higher cost in the long run. Ventilation is important too. A stuffy or cold atmosphere is not conducive to encourage enthusiasm amongst personnel. Elsewhere in the book I discuss the idea of encouraging communicators to 'smile' over the telephone to their prospects. Someone who is too hot, too cold, straining their eyes or has backache is going to have problems in making a minimum number of calls, never mind smiling!

As the 'no smoking' rule is a basic requirement in a telephone marketing atmosphere, it is particularly important to provide an area where the communicator can get a hot or cold drink and, if need be, have a cigarette. Some companies find that an allowance of a 20-minute break in every three-hour shift is adequate; most today believe, as I do, that communicators can slip off to have a drink whenever they wish at any time; and that smoking should be confined to the lunch break.

Whichever options you choose, don't be tempted to cut down on the working conditions you provide. Apart from the actual telephone, your staff are your basic tool of trade.

Conclusion

Telephone marketing brings human resources and technology together. It is not a production line, and a good department should reflect this in the enthusiasm and concern of its personnel. Motivation by use of incentives and correct ergonomics is an integral part of the structure which is justified by substantially higher production through enthusiastic participation by the communicators.

7

Lists: what is available for telephone marketers

However wonderful your product or service, it will remain on the shelf if you can't find the consumer to buy it. Lists are at the very core of the telephone marketing industry.

The very best list you will ever have is the one that is already in your files – your existing customers. The next most successful should be your file of lapsed customers, with the enquirees who have not yet proceeded to order as third in line. Telephone marketing to all three of these categories will not only keep them 'live' but can reactivate the second and re-motivate the third category in a highly cost-effective manner. We all like to visit where we feel most welcome. A *maitre d'hotel* of a good restaurant has the right idea. He flatters us by remembering our name and by personally welcoming us to the establishments. When we leave he thanks us for our custom. The result is that we will go back time and again to that same restaurant. Exactly the same reaction can be achieved by telephone marketing. Flatter your customers and prospects by contacting them by name; emphasize the value you place on their custom – and there is every likelihood that you will achieve your objective.

Of course your existing file of names and addresses is not sufficient to obtain new business. It is essential therefore to produce an exact profile of your average customer – and use this as a base for acquiring further lists.

Once you have defined your target group, draw as broad a marketing outline as possible, and seek the help of responsible list brokers in order to identify those lists most likely to meet with your requirements.

There are many good publications available which provide a fair amount of information on businesses. We find that Kompass, published by Kompass Publishers, is very useful, and contains details on nearly 50,000 companies in the UK.

Individual names are provided of chairmen, directors, sales/ marketing, management and purchasing staff.

Similar directories are also available for most European countries.

Testing lists

Whatever degree of trust you place upon the list broker, do test lists at every point in the campaign, analyzing the variables in terms of timing, area, socio-economic groupings and approach. An investment in time and money in testing a list is always very worthwhile. Don't be tempted into a 'roll out' situation after an initial good response. Conversely don't disregard a file because the first few reactions have been disappointing. One of the main benefits of telephone marketing, as opposed to direct mail or any other media, is the ease and immediacy of testing.

After making a decision to use a particular list, you must always bear in mind that telephone marketing is a numbers game. The more calls you make, the more prospects and subsequent sales you will achieve; and a substantial allowance has to be made for sufficient numbers to be available for engaged signals, gone aways and heavy call-back situations.

Out of every 30 diallings, my company expects to make between seven and ten contacts for industrial promotions, and between ten and 15 for consumer campaigns (dependent of course upon the accuracy of the information in the file being used).

One of the many advantages of using the telephone to market your product is that you can easily and quickly test not only the script, but also the actual list before you start to roll out.

To quote an example: a mail order company purchased a large quantity of good quality suitcases. These were considered too up-market and expensive for their usual C1/C2 mailing list, and they decided to try and sell by a combination of telephone and mail to a completely 'cold' file. The first list they rented was a file of people who had booked a holiday cruise. The profile appeared to be the correct one, and it was decided that some 12,000 persons would be contacted, in a two-stage promotion.

Firstly by mailing-out an attractive folder; secondly by a telephone marketing call endeavouring to obtain an order. I persuaded the company to test the list beforehand and prior to the mailing, the telephone was used on a small sampling of 500 random names from the file. Two facts emerged immediately. The incidence of 'nixies' on the list was disproportionately high at over ten per cent and the prospects were unanimously not interested in the product. The main reason for this was that the list was made up primarily of first-time cruisers who had taken the trip within the previous two years, and on that occasion had bought new suitcases to embark with on their holiday.

As an alternative, the mail order company rented a list of people who were known to fly regularly. A similar 500 random test proved that the file was acceptably accurate with two per cent 'nixies' and the positive reaction to the proposal justified a roll-out situation, which in fact achieved a very satisfactory level of 6.3 per cent orders, against a break-even requirement of 2.5 per cent.

While it can be a mistake to be too selective, it is a much bigger mistake to rent large lists without first testing. There should not be any delay in testing by telephone, and very little cost. The availability of being able to 'put a toe into the water before jumping in' must be regarded as a bonus for every marketing director.

Geography can be an important factor. Suburban listings may produce better results than urban simply because shopping by post may be easier when there are longer distances to travel – and the local retail outlets may not have sufficient variety of merchandise. In other instances the reverse may be true.

Think carefully about the quantity of names you may need. There is little point in renting a list of 100,000 if you have only four communicators. By the time they reach the end of the file, it will necessarily be out-of-date.

The direct mail industry has always been conscious of the problem of unwanted mail and in March 1983 a mail preference scheme was set up. Members of the public are invited to write in using Freepost 22, and receive in return a full explanation of the service. In five years only 80,000 individuals have asked to have their names removed from mailing lists; and a surprising 11,000 requests have been received from members of the public who have actually asked for their names and addresses to be added on to the files of all subscribing members.

With their thoughts turning in the same direction, the telephone committee of the British Direct Marketing Association are discussing the formation of a similar scheme. Individuals who make known their objections to any form of telephone solicitation will have the opportunity of asking to have their details removed from the files of subscribing telephone bureaux. Obviously, there will also be the opportunity to request an 'add-on' to all appropriate files.

The following is a selection of list brokers and lists currently being offered with telephone numbers, subject of course to the individual company's conditions of contract and availability. (Their inclusion in this book in no way implies a recommendation of the lists as particularly suitable or successful for any particular project.)

KPA Direct Marketing
16–18 Wadsworth Rd
Greenford, Middx UB6 7JL
01-991 2515
Business to business lists. 900 lists of which approximately 600 have 50–90 per cent telephone number availability.

Reed Database
Quadrant Hse
The Quadrant, Sutton, Surrey SM2 5AS
01-661 3355
Approximately 200,000 UK companies' information from Kompass, Kelly's Business Directory, Kelly's Post Office London Business Directory, Directory of Directors, British Exports. All telephone numbers available.

Resource Data Marketing Ltd
2 Station Parade
Ashford, Middx TW15 2RX
0784 240400
Specialist list builders. Offer both business and consumer lists. Telephone numbers not available with home addresses.

Mailist Ltd
1 Whiteladies Rd
Clifton
Bristol BS8 1NU
0272 737763
Business lists with telephone numbers available on request.

Benn Business Information Services Ltd
Sovereign Way
Tonbridge, Kent TN9 1RQ
Business lists with telephone numbers. Geographical breakdown is available by county.

Business Lists UK
4 Gilbert Rd
Cheadle Hulme
Cheadle, Ches SK8 6NB
Business lists. 80–90 per cent have phone numbers.

Yellow Pages Business Data
77/83 The Broadway
W. Ealing
London W13 9BP
01-567 7300
Telephone numbers available. Named managing director and financial director available.

Dun & Bradstreet
26–32 Clifton St
London EC2
01-377 4377
Industrial and commercial lists available. Approximately 90 per cent of lists have telephone numbers available on a database of 400,000.

Eagle Mailing Ltd
245/7 Redcatch Rd
Knowle, Bristol BS4 2HQ
0272 772240
UK & N. Ireland Business lists. Very broad base of titles. Large
percentage with telephone numbers.

Ibis Information Services
Waterside
Lowbell Lane
London Colney, St Albans, Herts AL2 1DX
0727 25209
This organization offers a database of 130,000 companies,
available geographically with 80 per cent named individuals; 95
per cent have telephone numbers.

A very useful source of information is the current British
Directories compiled by CBD Research Ltd, 15 Wickham Road,
Beckenham, Kent BR3 2JS. Telephone 01-650 7745. Thousands
of directories are sourced by subject – an invaluable aid to
obtaining lists. The same organization publishes a Directory of
European Professional and Learned Societies in 34 independent
states of Europe, giving valuable data about many lists available.

Timing

Failure of a campaign to succeed may not be because of the list.
The timing of your telephone calls must be carefully studied and
based not only on an evaluation of the original test, but also on
knowledge of outside influences. There is, for example, very
little point in telephoning a GP during the morning when he is in
his surgery, or contacting a company director at 6 pm on a
Friday when he is anxious to get home for the weekend.
Conversely, there is every reason to believe that you are likely to
reach a high incidence of farmers at 5.30 pm on a winter's
evening, or be able to contact school teachers at their homes
during school holidays.
  A great deal of thought should be given to the lifestyle of the

prospect. You may well be self-defeating in promulgating a programme of telephone marketing to parents of infants, if your telephone marketers make contact between 6 and 7.30 pm when the parent is particularly busy putting the children to bed. At the same time you can irritate the man of the house if you telephone during the Cup Final, or some other shattering world event! It is not always possible to be aware of these circumstances, particularly in cases where the campaign is directed universally rather than to one location, but the keen supervisor should pick up on the situation quickly and will wisely call a halt to the promotion.

Duplication

Avoid duplication like the plague. Nothing annoys a prospect more than to be called twice, unless it is (horror of horrors) to be called more than twice. If your list comes off the computer, your own or anybody else's, make sure that it has been run through the de-duplication programme, not only for the exact name and address, but also taking out more than one different name at the *same* address and telephone number. Nowadays it is not unusual for two people to live together, unmarried but as one household, and two telephone calls are almost never justified in those circumstances. The situation must be particularly looked at when a list is split between various communicators, who would not have any means of realizing that the prospect had already been contacted.

Random dialling

Random or sequential dialling is used a great deal in the USA, and to a degree by certain direct sales companies here. It is hazardous and not to be recommended either ethically or in terms of achieving a successful campaign.

Subscribers who go to the trouble of ensuring their numbers are not listed in the telephone directories do not regard telephone solicitations favourably – and such calls would kindle a reaction which it is in all the industry's interests to avoid.

On the subject of random dialling by machine, Sir Gordon

Borrie, Director General of Fair Trading, commented in the OFT Report on Telephone Selling published in October 1984:

British Telecom has confirmed that it remains opposed to the use of random or sequential call diallers on the grounds that this would place an intolerable burden on the existing cable network.

The Office therefore remains strongly opposed to the introduction of automatic dialling equipment in the UK unless there are adequate facilities to enable people to avoid receiving such calls should they so wish.

The BDMA's telephone committee unanimously agreed with the importance of this comment, and the guidelines contain a firm commitment to the sentiments expressed on this subject by the Office of Fair Trading.

8

Scriptwriting

Script? Oh no, not for us, we don't want our communicators to speak parrot fashion!

Quite right. You don't. Let's make it quite clear from the outset that a script is to be used as a *guideline* – not as a straitjacket. It is meant to be a help, and ought never to be a sacrosanct document to be kept to at all costs, word-for-word.

We've all watched admiringly as the best of our stage and TV actors and actresses manage to ad-lib 'perfectly', i.e. to suit the mood of the audience and the needs of that special moment. The most skilful always seem to radiate warmth and sympathy. Well, that's the way it ought to be with a telephone communicator too. The script is necessary to make sure the most salient points have been covered and the meaning of the message remains the same – but it needs to allow flexibility. It has to give your best communicators freedom to 'ad-lib'.

That freedom also extends to particular phrases within the script.

Because all people are – thank heavens! – different, some of them will find difficulty in saying particular phrases. Forcing them to utter these puts them right into that 'straitjacket'.

Take, as an example, that American way of ending a conversation with 'Have a nice day!' It so happens that I personally find it particularly pleasant, but I do know that our own communicators feel embarrassed by it. Asking them to use the phrase would be just ridiculous. They don't feel right about saying 'Have a nice day!', and, because of this, they would distort the words and meaning.

The point of 'Have a nice day!' is, after all, to end a conversation pleasantly, and that can be done with a phrase which British communicators find more 'natural'. So long as the conversation ends pleasantly, it doesn't matter, after all, how the call is terminated – whether it's with 'Have a nice day', or 'Well, I'll say goodbye and thanks', or even simply by, 'Thank you for your time'.

The point is, once again, to make sure your script allows for flexibility. Demanding anything else is not only silly, but unrealistic too. Even if you did insist your communicators stuck to the script, they would deviate from it after the first hour or so, finding phrases they felt were more 'natural' to them.

Scriptwriters and word-pictures

The playwright Luigi Pirandello once wrote, 'Six Characters in Search of an Author'. In just the same way, your communicators – and the message they're meant to communicate – are in urgent need of an 'author' – a scriptwriter. So where do you find one? And who is likely to be a good scriptwriter?

Let's begin by weeding out those who won't fit the bill. They include a lot of people who might be regarded as logical candidates for the job. But, without special training, the following *won't* qualify:

● your direct mail copywriter;
● your advertising agency's copywriter;
● your company's star marketing and/or sales director; and
● that clever fellow or girl who usually writes your company's sales pitches

The fact is that a scriptwriter has to be trained in the fine art of producing word-pictures. A moment's thought will show you that this is a very special writing – and selling – skill.

Any form of writing other than scriptwriting can be accompanied by an illustration or picture of the product. Much the same is true for other forms of selling. Your salesperson can produce samples, take a prospect to a demonstration, or at the very least show a leaflet. Moreover, the salesperson has the added benefit of using facial expressions, gestures, even bodily attitudes ('body language') to illustrate and emphasize the points being made.

The telephone communicator has only words.

Let's see what those words have to do – the kind of job they're meant to perform.

In order to illustrate this, let us suppose for a moment that you, the reader, are office manager of a company employing, say, 75 staff, and that a salesman has called in at your firm's reception, asking to see you about 'Bloggs Photocopiers'.

You're not really very interested, but you agree to see the sales representative anyway, perhaps because you have a slack moment, or maybe because you feel you ought to keep abreast of what new photocopying equipment is available on the market.

The sales rep immediately makes a good impression. He has a nice appearance, a pleasant, honest face and you are quite impressed when, after firmly shaking your hand, he asks for permission to demonstrate the machine he has left in his car – entirely without obligation, of course. In due course he has set up the machine on a corner of a desk in your office, and you can see that it looks good and works well.

Understandably, however, you can't make up your mind then and there whether to buy it or not, and so you ask the rep to call again after you and others in your company have given the matter some further consideration.

That sales call has probably cost Bloggs Photocopiers Limited around £70.

A telephone call could have achieved the same level of interest in the product and ensured a definite appointment for a demonstration at a *fraction* of the cost. Moreover, an appointment arranged by telephone would certainly have put the onus on the prospect to proceed with the purchase.

In order to accomplish this, however, your telephone communicators would have needed to use a script which provided an attractive word picture – one which would have had to be painted something like this:

The Bloggs Photocopier is an ultra-modern machine, beautifully designed and finished smoothly in aluminium painted silver grey . . . It's so compact that, at just 18 inches by 18 inches, it can sit at the end of anybody's desk . . . and it's so easy to use that even the errand boy can run it without any problems at all.

Making the negatives pay off

Selling by telephone demands a re-think of your sales techniques and even of your product. Why, for example, do your salesmen get turned down – when they do? What arguments do they encounter most frequently? What are the chief objections they hear, time and time again?

Take a full briefing from your company's salespeople. They are, after all, the ones most deeply involved in your product or services. They're the troops on the firing-line, the ones who receive all the 'flak'. It's the job of management to know what that 'flak' consists of.

Your salespeople can provide you with a list of the reasons prospects give for not placing an order. These reasons are ammunition for you. They're the 'objections' you need to incorporate into your script, along with the answers most likely to convert them into a sale. If a company has a large sales force, so much the better; management should talk to as many sales representatives as possible, and then collate all the information they provide.

At the end of the exercise, you should end up with a paper which looks like this:

Objection	Positive response
'We've already got a photocopier.'	Yes, but the Bloggs machine is so inexpensive it will pay you to have another one in your office.
'The budget for this quarter has been spent.'	In that case I suggest we reserve a machine at today's price and deliver to you, say, May 1st?
'I'll never have another Bloggs! Our last Bloggs machine kept breaking down.'	Yes, but that was before we developed the model 73X. Over 1,500 machines have been installed without complaint. Quite a record don't you agree!

| 'We'll think it over and let you know.' | May I suggest that you reconsider and place your order now, as there is a once-only discount of 15 per cent which is only available till the end of this month. |

And so on and so forth. While the objections are not strictly part of the script, they have to be readily and immediately available on a separate document or flip-chart, so that the telephone communicator can refer to them easily.

Fourteen basic scriptwriting rules

1 *Communicators must be treated as actors*
Each communicator must be an actor: delivering a polished performance after rehearsal; making every presentation a memorable occasion for his/her audience. Communicators have to be trained for their roles so that they develop a method of approach which will reflect their individual personality, yet maintaining the ability to incorporate the important 'buzz words' in any script. Scripts must be designed with this in mind, with the important words and phrases highlighted.

2 *Talk to the right person*
The opening gambit should always be directed at making certain that the voice at the other end of the telephone belongs to the key person – the decision-maker.

3 *Be open and above board*
Telephone communicators should introduce themselves by name, detail the company they represent, and briefly indicate the purpose of the call being made.

4 *Use the first twenty–thirty seconds effectively*
Remember always that communicators have only 20–30 seconds to state the purpose of the call. Ensure, therefore, that the initial introduction will rivet the attention of the recipient by suggesting the worthwhile benefits to him.

74

5 *Let the prospect comment*

The script should allow for plenty of pauses, giving the recipient of the call an opportunity to make comments and allowing the telephone communicator a chance to estimate the initial reaction. Remember: pauses are not hesitatons!

6 *Soft-sell*

In order to establish a rapport with the prospect and to ensure his or her cooperation in allowing the conversation to continue, always obtain permission beforehand. A very effective way of doing this is to use the opening phrase, 'May I just have sixty seconds of your time to tell you about . . . ? My experience proves that very few people refuse to listen for just one minute, and that is enough time for a communicator to project a 150-word story about a product or service.

7 *Word pictures*

This is the point where your 'word-pictures' come in – coupled with the 'benefits' to the prospect. It is quite helpful when initially writing scripts to dictate these benefits and those word pictures onto a tape, then to play the tape back while you shut your eyes and imagine yourself at the receiving end of such a conversation. The benefit *to the prospect* must be told at the beginning of the script.

8 *Give your communicator the chance to listen*

Your script should provide for pauses to allow your telephone communicator to gauge reactions, and then either continue with the call plan if the response has been positive or allow the communicator to refer to his or her 'objections' sheet, if a negative answer has been received.

9 *Make it positive*

The script should always allow for definite affirmative responses. Instead of saying, 'Would you like a representative to call upon you next week, Mr Brown?', the script should be re-phrased to put the question this way: 'Which day of the week would suit you best, Mr Brown – Monday, Tuesday, Wednesday, Thursday or Friday? Or are weekends more convenient for you?'

In the same way, whenever you are direct selling, always assume the larger quantity. In other words, rather than saying, 'How many would you like?', say, 'I am sure you will want to take advantage of the 20 per cent discount we offer on 12 gross packs, Mr Brown.'

Make sure to leave little opportunity for the recipient of your call to say 'no'. Always give positive alternatives: 'Is it 12 gross or 24 gross, Mr Brown?' and 'Would Thursday or Friday be a better evening for the kitchen furniture salesmen to call, Mrs Smith?'

10 *Help the prospect come to a decision*

Communicators should always bear in mind that the prospect may not be aware of a need for the product until the benefits are highlighted. To be 'pushy' or aggressive can cause irreparable damage. Signals must be read carefully and translated into the kind of help to which the prospect can relate.

11 *Keep to the point*

The commitment to a time, quantity, or request for a brochure is really the close of a script. Do not overextend this! The lengthier you make a script, the more chance you stand of losing the attention of the listener, and the less time the telephone communicator has to make the next call.

Don't get too involved in trying to explain all the whys and wherefores of the product or service you offer, or attempt to detail very involved pricing structures, where for example you are offering various models. The aim of the script on these occasions should only be to gain the interest of the prospect and his or her agreement to receive a detailed catalogue, or make a firm appointment for your salesperson to visit.

Leave plenty of room for comments. All good telephone selling should have a strong element of a research questionnaire in it. If the answer is 'no', make sure you find out *why*.

Write the script in the same way as you would talk to a new acquaintance to whom you were hoping to sell. Eliminate any phrases which make your pitch sound phoney. Cut down on the effervescence. Comments such as 'I am absolutely delighted to speak to you' impress no one and are usually immediately rejected by the prospect.

12 *Ask the right questions*
When planning your script, make sure that your initial questions give a good opportunity to your trained telephone communicator to probe, so that he or she will quickly learn from the responses received whether there is a qualified prospect at the other end of the phone.

13 *Have at least two objectives*
A call need not necessarily be 'wasted' if the primary objective is not immediately achieved. Leave room within the script for lesser objectives.

For example, if the prospect is not interested in placing an order for the six shirts you hope to sell him, leave the way open to send him a catalogue and get permission for a further call to be made after he has had a chance to look through it.

14 *Testing*
One of the bonuses in telephone marketing is that it provides a company with the ability to test and test and test again. The telephone is the one medium in which you do not have to stay with failure – unlike radio and television commercials or print media, where once you have placed your advertising message, you have to live with it.

Testing extensively by telephone is *not* costly. After a good writer has completed the first draft of a script, you can select 100 names at random from a proposed list of targets, and then get your best telephone communicator to make contact with these, using the initial script. Analyzing the reaction will determine what, if any, alterations are needed in the script, and this is a process which should continue until a satisfactory set of responses is received.

The section that follows looks at some typical scripts and telephone marketing situations. In each case, the scripts cover a different area, but all are actual. They have all been used successfully and each has been developed after careful initial testing.

You may think that the product or service you offer is too technical to be sold by phone. This might indeed be the case – but *only* if you are trying to 'cold sell' a highly technical product. If, on the other hand, you use the two or three-stage approach described in Chapter 11, 'The winning combination', then it is *not* impossible. Take the case of a company promoting the sale of air compressors – not an easy product to promote, as you'll agree. Yet a *very* successful three-stage telephone/direct mail/telephone campaign was conducted, using the following script (into which I have incorporated instructions to the telephone communicator using it):

Three-stages: telephone, mail, telephone

Stage 1: Initial telephone call

Good morning/afternoon, may I please speak to the person within your company who would specify the purchase of air compressors?

At contact: Good morning/afternoon, Mr Brown, my name is Paul Jones, calling on behalf of the XYZ Company about our range of special air compressors and ancillary equipment. We will be sending your company some information about this and would like to confirm that you are the correct person with whom to liaise.
(If not, find out who the correct person is and repeat.)

Use long distance as a reason

If you are calling outside your town, mention this fact as a reason for being connected quickly. 'This is Paul Jones calling long distance for Mr Brown. Can you put me through right away, please?'

Overcome unavailability

If the person you want is at a meeting, or otherwise engaged, get an indication of a time when he or she will be available and make sure you call back then. 'I am phoning Mr Brown at this time, as we arranged. . . .'

When endeavouring to reach business executives it is essential to develop these persistent formulas in order to obtain maximum exposure to the key decision-makers.

Telephone sales techniques of course vary, according to the needs of the programme.

An example is provided by a holiday group which wished to sell their programmes directly into working men's clubs and associations. As these 4,000 clubs are spread sparsely up and down the country, the cost of sending a sales force was obviously uneconomical particularly as club and association secretaries, or organizers, are usually available only during very limited periods throughout the year.

The holiday group turned to telephone marketing and a very successful phonesell exercise resulted, despite the fact that it was necessary to make as many as three or four call-backs to contact the correct person.

Figure 9 shows the script I provided for our telephone communicators in this exercise. Out of a total of 4,000 clubs and associations, my company contacted 3,500 club secretaries and organizers. Of these, 81 per cent agreed to receive information. We have been advised by our client, 'XYZ Company', that conversions to solid bookings exceed ten per cent.

Total cost: £12,250
Total bookings for current year of exercise: £320,000 – with the added benefit of a roll-on situation for subsequent annual bookings.

Stage 2: Personalized direct mail is then sent to the named specifiers

Stage 3: Second telephone call

Good morning Mr Brown, this is Paul Jones of the XYZ Company. I recently fulfilled a promise to send you some information about our special air compressors.
(Pause for comment.)

Our technical representative would like to call and discuss the benefits of the product in greater detail. Can I arrange that he calls upon you Monday of next week, or would you prefer Tuesday/Wednesday/ Thursday/Friday, am or pm:
(If negative, probe.)

Is it for budgetary reasons you do not wish to see a technical representative, Mr Brown. XYZ operate a very economical leasing scheme, which coupled with the advanced technology of our new equipment, is guaranteed to save you money.
(Refer to list of objections and responses.)

Overcoming the secretarial hurdle

The vast majority of secretaries and PAs zealously guard their bosses. After all, this is part of their job, and the following techniques are useful in order to penetrate the screen they throw around their employers.

If you're following a mailing campaign

Refer to the correspondence; 'I'm calling Mr Brown to discuss the letter I recently sent him.'

Assertively

If the secretary insists on finding out your reasons for wanting to talk to her boss, be assertive: 'I feel sure Mr Brown would wish me to talk directly to him.'

By-pass the barrier

Many executives start work earlier than their employees. If you try an early morning or late afternoon call, you may well get through directly.

Look again at question 6a, where the communicator is asked to probe the reason why the prospect doesn't want literature. The reason could be anything. Maybe he just doesn't understand the offer being made to him. That, too, happens. A few probing questions and a presentation of benefits can alter an attitude and promote a desire to learn more about the product or service the telephone communicator is offering.

Probe: 'Exactly why aren't you interested in our holiday package?'

Objection: 'I've heard uncomplimentary things about your company.'

Reply: 'Our company? I find that incredible!'

Figure 9 Sample script

---

1 You will be speaking to working men's clubs/associations. Ask for *the person responsible for organizing trips and holidays for members*:

Contact name, including initials _____

Title _____

2 'Good afternoon/evening. My name is ____ and I am calling on behalf of the XYZ Holiday Group. I understand, Mr (contact name), that you are responsible for organizing trips and holidays for your members. Is that correct?' (yes/no)

3 'Have you ever used XYZ before?' (yes/no)

4 (If 'yes') 'Oh good! Then you must be aware. . . .'
(If 'no') 'That's a shame! Well, then perhaps you are not aware. . . .'

5 '. . . (aware/not aware) that XYZ is able to offer you holiday and leisure facilities which can be tailor-made to suit your requirements – either just for an individual member or for a group – and for the length of time you require.'

6 'I would like to send some information for you to look at showing our exciting programmes.' (Pause for comment).
a (If negative) Probe reason and offer benefits.
b (If positive) 'As we have so much to offer, and just to make sure that the literature I will be sending you deals with your specific needs, I should like to take just 30 seconds of your time with some brief questions:
  ● How many members do you have?
  ● How many usually join the holiday scheme?
  ● Where have you travelled to these last three years?
  ● What sort of holiday is most popular?
  ● What time of year is preferred?
  ● How much per head would you expect to pay?'

7 Thank him for his time and promise to put the literature in the post promptly

---

The communicator has now established the reason why the prospect refuses out of hand to see the material being offered. If a probing question had not been asked the call would have been wasted and a sale lost indefinitely.

Any objection must always be answered immediately, even if it is only by means of a paraphrase of the prospect's own words.

Objection: 'You're too expensive.'
Reply: 'We're too expensive'.

Objection: 'There's no choice in your catalogue.'
Reply: 'You're saying there's no choice in *our* catalogue:'

Following the immediate response, the communicator must launch into the benefits, all of which should be separately listed and easily identified.

Objection	*Benefit*
'Your holidays are too expensive.'	'Compared with any of our rivals, we offer better prices £ for £ for quality accommodation.'
'We don't want to travel up to Heathrow Airport.'	'Of course not. Our packages can be arranged from your local airport. That's Manchester, isn't it?'

Every telephone marketing campaign should be prepared on the basis that there will be objections from the prospects. Every communicator must be prepared to overcome these objections at any time during the entire course of the conversation. There are, however, occasions when probing reveals that there is little likelihood of converting the prospect to a customer, and it should be stressed to the communicators that it is far cheaper on those occasions to thank the person at the other end of the receiver for their time and politely end the call.

What's in it for the prospect

It must be borne in mind that the prospect is only interested in the benefit to himself or to his company if he proceeds to buy your product.

The following case history used this premise very successfully.

The object of the exercise was to induce stationery retailers to sell a particular brand of typewriter. The form given to the interviewer is shown in Figure 10.

As a result of this telephone sales campaign 1,000 retailers were contacted at a total cost of £3,500. Of these 206 agreed to make firm timed appointments to see the representative with a view to considering stocking the typewriters.

Figure 10 Sample script

(At first contact) 'Good morning/afternoon. May I please have the name of your managing director-buyer?'

Name and initials _____

Position _____

(On connection) 'Good morning/afternoon, Mr (contact name). My name is Paul Jones and I am calling on behalf of the Customer Services Division of XYZ Typewriter Co.'

1 'Do you sell typewriters from your premises?' (yes/no)
(If 'yes', continue)
(If 'no') 'well, I am surprised you don't sell typewriters, but I understand you do sell office equipment and stationery products. That's correct, isn't it?'

2 *(After response, continue)* 'If we could show you a way to sell typewriters profitably I am sure that you would be interested.'
(Pause for comment.)

---

3 'As you may be aware, Mr (contact name), from surveys taken within our industry, XYZ Tyepwriter Company will sell one out of every four typewriters sold in the UK this year. And on top of that, six out of every ten electric compacts and portables sold are sold by XYZ Typewriter Company. So obviously, if you aren't currently stocking XYZ typewriters, you are missing a great profit opportunity.

'Later this month, we're starting a major national advertising and promotion campaign costing over £500,000 which is going to prove very profitable to you if you participate. Mr Green, our Area Manager, has asked me to call you personally as he has not yet had the chance to meet you and explain the advantages to you of this vast campaign. He is in your area next *(day 1)* and *(day 2)* and has asked me to call you to check which of these days would be more suitable for you to meet him.

'Do you have your diary in front of you?'
'Which would you prefer, Mr (contact name?) (day 1) or (day 2)?

Appt. _____ Day _____ Date _____ Month _____ Time _____

(Repeat) 'So that is (time) o'clock, on (day) of (month). Now, just to make sure that Mr Green brings along the relevant information on the promotion for your particular business, may I just ask you some brief questions?

Q1: If they sell XYZ typewriters at present, ask 'Who is your current wholesaler?'

Q2: 'Which typewriters do you sell at present?'
(manufacturers)

1 _____

2 _____

3 _____

4 _____

5 _____

Phrases that make phoneselling easier

Simple phrases can make all the difference in detailing benefits and features. Here are some of the best:

Because it has. . . .
And this will give you. . . .
I'd like personally to tell you about. . . .
Not only . . . but also. . . .
Even though . . . we can still offer you. . . .
Additionally. . . .
Incredibly, we can still maintain. . . .

Closing a sale over the phone

There are four different ways of closing a sale:

1 *Direct*: 'May I confirm your name and address so that the order will be delivered *correctly*?'

2 *Assumptive*: 'Did you want three white shirts, Mr Brown, or have you decided to take three of the blue as well?'

3 *Optional*: 'Could Mr Green call on Monday at around 10 o'clock, or would you prefer to see him on another day? Perhaps Wednesday or Thursday?'

4 *Deferred*: 'I'm grateful for your interest and time, Mr Brown. Which day would you like me to call back so that you can confirm your order?'

It is important to develop techniques of knowing exactly when to close a presentation and to recognize the buying signals. It is a matter of listening very carefully to what is being said at the other end of the telephone.

Here are some examples of responses which are signalling that it is the correct time to close:

1 When the prospect responds by showing interest in your presentation:

It is time we thought about a microcomputer. . . . Our systems are rather out-of-date. . . .
It is time we looked at our policies again. . . .

2 If the prospect asks questions:

Do you have it in different colours?
What are the terms of payment?
Are there any leasing arrangements?

The script shown in Figure 11 was used in approaching housewives with the object of their becoming agents for a mail order company:

As a result of this campaign a very encouraging ten per cent of those receiving 'cold calls' expressed an interest in becoming agents.

Figure 11 Sample script

'Good morning/Evening, Ms Smith. This is Pamela Jones of XYZ Mail Order.'
1 'Have you seen any of our recent advertising? (yes/no)
(If 'yes', go to Question 2)
(If 'no') 'Well, as you probably know, we are a reputable and long-established catalogue mail order company, and we advertise in the national papers and women's magazines.'
2 'May I ask if you have any knowledge of mail order?' (yes/no)
(If 'no', go to Question 3)
(If 'yes') 'Do you actually run a catalogue? Have you thought of applying for a copy of ours?' (yes/no)
(If 'yes' go to question 4)
(If 'no' go to question 3)

3 'I am sure you would be interested in knowing a little more about how profitable the XYZ Mail Order Catalogue could be for you.' *(Pause for comment.)*
'Apart from the convenience of mail order fashion shopping, the credit facilities and the fact that you get ten per cent commission on everything you sell and of course buy for yourself means a *welcome extra income for you*, of course. Some of our agents earned as much as £800 in two months before Christmas, as well as getting a regular income throughout the year.'

4 'If you think you might be interested in running a catalogue, may I just ask if you are over 18 years of age?'
(If 'yes' go to question 5)
(If 'no') 'Do you have any friends or relatives who are over 18 and might be interested in having a catalogue? Then you could choose goods from the catalogue too.' (yes/no)
(If under 18) 'I'm sorry, we can't appoint an agent who is under 18, but I hope you will contact us when you reach 18. Thank you very much for your time, Ms Smith. Goodnight.'

5 'May I ask your local XYZ mail order representative to call with a copy of the catalogue for you to see?' (yes/no)
(If 'yes') 'What is the most convenient time for you? Thank you very much for your time, Mrs Smith. Your local representative will be in touch with you in the next few days. Goodnight.'
(If 'no') 'We can arrange to send a catalogue and application form by post if you prefer, but usually we find that people who are thinking of becoming an XYZ agent find it very helpful to chat with their local representative, who can answer any queries you may have and offer some useful advice on how to run an agency successfully.
(If still 'no') 'Very well, Mrs Smith, we'll be very happy to put a catalogue and application form in the post to you, together with a leaflet which explains some of the benefits you could enjoy as an XYZ agent. Thank you very much for your time. Goodnight.'

Overcoming resistance

A good communicator will not need to be a Sherlock Holmes in order to spot and interpret the clues he gets. Any of the following responses are a sure sign of resistance to the product or service being offered:

1 *Negative comments*
'I've never liked that firm.'
'It's too big to fit on my desk.'

'I've had one before and it was no good.'
'Can't see the need for one.'
'Much too expensive.'

2 *Silence*

No response to any pauses.

3 *Lack of interest*

'Oh yes!'
'Maybe.'
'Perhaps'
'If you say so.'
'All right . . . OK. . . . Uh-huh . . . etc., etc.,

4 *Doubts*

'I wouldn't have thought so.'
'Do you *really* believe that?'
'I don't agree.'

5 *Dissembling*

'Call me back another time.'
'I'll have to ask my wife/husband/boss, etc.'
'I must think about it.'

While recognition of actual resistance is quickly learned, it is more difficult to gauge how to identify the real underlying reasons for the prospect's resistance. Until you do this, you will not be able to sell to him or her.

The way to throw light on the hidden reasons for the objection is to ask questions – in fact, to go back to the technique of *probing*. Good opening phrases following resistance are:

- 'The special features of this are of course obvious to a man in your position, Mr Brown.'

- 'You do understand all the advantages, such as A, B, and C, don't you, Mr Brown?'

This will give Mr Brown the chance to talk a little more, and for the communicator to have an opportunity of realizing and over-coming the many obstacles.

Resolving resistance

	Solve the problem
1 A cash flow problem.	We can offer you a very low rate over a three–five year period.
	Open new ideas
2 We don't need a fax machine. We only send one message a day, and use a local bureau.	Our new model will enable you to have the message sent at night at the lowest rates and you will probably find that it will be cheaper and faster to have the convenience of your own fax.
	Give proof
3 I understand your service department is really slow and very expensive.	In the last six years we have sold 20,000 microwaves and have only had 200 service calls. 150 of these were made within 24 hours without any charge to the consumer.
	Redirect attention
4 32K is much too small I'm told for my accounting needs.	Our new accounting programme is better than anything else available on the market and used by many of your competitors.
	Deny strongly
5 I expect you charge for every single extra that you can: deliveries and so forth.	No Mr Brown: XYZ make it a policy to have no 'hidden costs' at all.

Third party referral

6 Everybody in the trade
   seems to order from your
   competitors, the ABC
   Company.

By no means, Mr Brown.
Hardings, a *very* successful
company as you know, only
order from us and in fact have
doubled up on last year.

Always bear in mind that resistance does not necessarily crop up
in the middle or the end of a presentation. Resistance can be
there from the very inception of the call.

As an example, the prospect could say, 'XYZ Company? No
thank you, I've had very poor service from you in the past.' This
of course is an example of resistance which must be overcome
before the presentation carries on.

Always set a call plan beforehand in conjunction with the
script and provide the communicators with ancillary material
and details of the reasons why your products or services are
better than anything else available.

Before commencing a new script, ensure that a full briefing
takes place and the key words are noted. These will always
include the benefits to the prospect as well as other advantageous features. The value and strength of the key words and
phrases must be emphasized to the communicators – as well as
the dangers of omitting them from the 'sales pitch'.

9

Creating and handling incoming calls

As recently as three years ago, filling out and posting off a coupon was the only direct response way of applying for mail order goods, brochures, information packs and booking theatre tickets. The situation completely altered with the wide distribution of credit cards, and the use of TV advertisements to promote *incoming* telephone numbers. Organizations such as Teledata with their 200-0-200 numbers were among the first in this field, and British Telecom themselves were soon to realize the potential of this type of business, and opened their own incoming call handling company in Bristol.

Most consumers do not have any objection to writing off for something which has caught their interest. By the time, however, that they have torn the advertisement out of the publication, found a pen, filled in the coupon, acquired an envelope and a stamp, and remembered to drop it into the letterbox, many of them will have become distracted from their original purchasing purpose. Often too, lethargy or lack of time means that the envelope never gets addressed, let alone actually posted. The coupons which have been cut out are put aside for attention at a later date – and then forgotten. Picked up again after a few days have lapsed, they are often discarded, because the earlier enthusiasm isn't there any more.

Organizations who use telephone numbers in their advertisements, side by side with the usual name and address panel, find that they can receive up to *five and a half times more response* from phone enquiries than they do from the post. Conversions too are usually higher. The time lapse between making a call and receiving a brochure is much shorter than posting a coupon and waiting for a response. Indeed, the use of the phone speeds up everything and boosts sales and cash flow dramatically. An oft-quoted saying in the direct mail business is, 'The first brochure in your hand is the one you are most likely to purchase from.'

That's true enough – as the holiday tour operators well know – and by using the telephone to make their requests consumers receive their brochures that much quicker. An added plus for the advertiser is that having achieved a voice-to-voice contact, the prospect is now much more aware of the company's existence and a pleasant reception from the voice at the other end of the phone is an added inducement when considering his purchase.

Incoming telephone call training is as important at outgoing. The incoming telephone communicator is a shop window for the company, either enticing the customer to come in and buy the goods, or putting up a barrier and providing reasons for the prospect to go elsewhere. Wanting the business is just not enough: pleasant and enthusiastic communicators trained to sell and to communicate the merchandise or service being offered by painting 'word pictures' are essential.

An incoming call communicator should not be just an 'order taker' but a trained salesperson who is fully conversant with stock positions, and the relative advantages of the items being sold. In exactly the same way as an outgoing call communicator, the incoming sales person must be able quickly and picturesquely to describe the benefits to the *prospect* rather than to the company doing the selling.

---

10 Rules for Inbound Communicators

1. Make your next call your best call whatever time of the day.

2. Answer the phone promptly by the third ring. Nothing tends to irritate a caller more than waiting to be answered.

3. Don't answer the phone whilst finishing a conversation or sharing a joke. Be happy; but make the caller feel that he has your entire attention.

4. Listen carefully to whatever is being said to you. If you're unfamiliar with a word or a description, don't guess at it – but ask politely for it to be repeated.

5. Taking down correct names and addresses is vital. Familiarize yourself with counties and main towns. Above all, be quite sure you have the post-code accurately transcribed.

6. Don't eat, drink, smoke or glance at your magazine whilst you are on the telephone. The caller needs your full attention.

7. If you need to ask the caller to 'hold on' whilst you obtain fuller information, make sure you keep him informed on what you are doing. Long silences are annoying to the caller and must be avoided.

8. Don't interrupt. The person at the other end of the line is all important. Let him have his say and show that his opinion or request is valued by the company you represent.

9. However irritating the person at the end of the phone is, your intelligence and professionalism must allow you to deal with him in a calm and courteous manner.

10. Watch your words. As a professional communicator you must talk smartly and positively. Phrases such as 'Yes. Certainly', are your business tools. Slang such as 'OKAY', 'SURE', 'RIGHT' are not conducive to good inbound communication.

Freephone

Although quite expensive for the advertiser, Freephone, is used effectively by many organizations. Mercedes Benz, for example, used it in promoting their truck division. Transport managers and interested prospects could ring the operator anywhere in Britain and by quoting Freephone Mercedes Benz be put in touch with a member of the company who provided immediate comprehensive information on the company's vehicles, and also arranged for a test drive at any appropriate dealer location. One of the advantages of Freephone is that it can be set up very quickly, and there is no need to make any commitment to a long-term contract.

RCF

An alternative to the Freephone system is the remote call forwarding service – RCF. This allows you to use local telephone numbers in any town in the country, and have the calls routed to your centre of operations. Consumers are often hesitant to make outside area calls because of the cost (and who can blame them) and this can seriously inhibit the effectiveness of a telephone direct response programme. If, however, the telephone number is a local one, the number of calls should increase substantially. Once the appropriate number has been dialled, the caller is answered with a recorded message explaining that they will be shortly connected with the advertiser. Of course, while the caller pays local charges only, the recipient pays the balance of the cost.

The main advantage of RCF is that it is both quick and easy to obtain, and enables the subscriber to have a telephone presence in locations away from its offices.

Toll-free 0800

Success in business, by maintaining a competitive edge, needs all the help you can get from the effective use of telecommunications to provide that all-important quality of service. The use of 0800 (named Linkline by British Telecom, but more commonly known by the American description of 'toll-free') makes customer contact attractive, effective, efficient and accountable.

Simple to use it encourages prospective and existing customers to call in to place an order, raise a query, get further particulars or talk about product.

What you may have to offer could be the ultimate in product or service, but if the action required in purchasing or accessing your service isn't straightforward, you will lose out to the competition.

No one likes to be criticized. However, most companies are becoming very willing, and indeed anxious, to listen to constructive criticism. Research has shown that consumers don't complain for the following reasons:

1   They can't find the correct telephone number
2   A letter is too much effort
3   Time needed to get to the 'correct person' to deal with their complaint
4   Cost of a telephone call

The installation of an 0800 toll-free number helps a company gain immediate feedback of purchasers' attitudes towards the product, and provides, at the same time, significant marketing implications.

With 50 per cent of all queries generally judged to be due to product misuse, the provision of a free 'hotline' must save considerably in providing a call-out service, while at the same time generating a more proficient use of the product – and therefore a higher degree of purchaser satisfaction.

0800 has now been around for a few years. After a successful trial by British Telecom in July 1985 with an original 20 customers, the facility is growing rapidly, as more and more firms realize the potential of providing the public with an 0800 number, followed by six digits, which they can dial directly – at no cost to themselves.

The same number can be used throughout the UK, which is advantageous when using it in conjunction with TV and national press. It should be stressed, however, that presentation of the telephone number itself is as important as placing the coupon correctly would have been in the days when a telephone toll-free number was not available. After all, ten digits is quite a lot to remember, and a quick flash in a ten-second commercial does not give the public much of an opportunity to note the number. Obviously, a 'good' telephone number is advantageous, and if using a bureau to handle the response, this should be one of the factors taken into account when you make your choice.

To maximize an 0800 promotion do make sure that the phones are answered by communicators who are trained as carefully as those who make outbound calls. Think of them in the same way you do of your reception. Certainly, you would not allow anybody who had a 'scruffy' appearance or indifferent voice or attitude to be the first person your prospects see when they enter your building. In the same way, when your 0800 number is answered, this may well be the first, and most lasting, impression that your prospects receive. 0800 numbers, like other forms of telephone marketing, can be answered in such a way that they immediately generate more sales – and indeed can be an ideal time for upselling.

The hotel groups, such as the Sheraton, were among the first to realize the potential in encouraging people to call in this way.

Sheraton Hotels took up Linkline 0800 as soon as it became available in the UK as they already used freephone throughout the rest of the world. They wanted to make it as easy as possible for anyone to reach them – not specifically business organizations. The 0800 number is advertised in upmarket magazines, travel trade papers and travel agents, and 75 per cent of their business is from the business traveller whom they contacted direct with mail shots to advise of their 0800 number, resulting in a marked increase in the number of calls.

On-the-ball organizations such as EFFEM, the largest producer of animal food in Germany, soon saw the potential, and used their equivalent Service 0130 to generate thousands of calls in response to a very creative and funny campaign on TV and in national magazines.

Autoglass, Britain's biggest replacement automotive glazing company, was one of the four pioneers of the 0800 system. With over 140 wholly-owned branches nationwide, speedy communication is vital for a company that replaces three quarters of a million pieces of glass each year.

Over 75 per cent of Autoglass's total business passes through the control centre at the company's Bedford headquarters with (currently) 27 operators taking calls on the 0800 363636 number.

Touch-screen computers allow the operators to call up all the necessary information to assist the customer and then work instructions are faxed through to the appropriate branch. Average response time to the 0800 number is under four seconds and most callers are dealt with, pleasantly and efficiently, in less than two minutes.

Calls to the single direct dial number are approximately 35,000 per week (and growing all the time); during the great storm of October 1987, no less than 30,000 calls for assistance were answered in one weekend.

Rank Xerox, whose principal strategic objective is customer satisfaction, make full use of 0800 as:

1 A single point of caller-orientated contact for customer enquiries by telephone in response to practically all of their direct marketing, advertising and PR activity and the professional, monitored and managed receipt, resolution or distribution of those customer enquiries.
2 A direct, easy-to-use, toll-free service which allows the customer to come straight through to the people equipped and trained to help at no expense.

With an 0800 number, a company can be accessed at all times and becomes highly visible. A case in point is The Mortgage Corporation. A totally centralized company with no retail outlets and no high street presence, the organization carries a prominent 0800 number in all of its advertising.

If the situation is such that the advertiser does not want to bear the full cost of the free 0800 call, the alternative 0345 also encourages public use. With the 0345 the caller pays local charges, while the advertiser pays the balance of the fee.

Some major credit card companies make particularly good use of the 0345 Linkline so that authorization calls from millions of outlets are only charged at the local rate. This reduces the time and cost for retailers, and provides the end users with additional protection against fraud.

International 0800

The business benefits of an International 0800 number are a way of increasing your international sales, without the heavy expenses incurred in setting up and staffing local offices to handle your business. Using toll-free, you can attract overseas business by making it easy for customers to contact you.

Prospective customers will be more likely to respond to your advertising if you provide a free opportunity to call. Often the cost is a barrier to large amounts of response; and, at the same time, using international toll-free also tells your prospective customers that you are a serious company.

INTERNATIONAL 0800 TOLL FREE

FINLAND
NORWAY
SWEDEN

DENMARK

JAPAN

HONG KONG

WEST GERMANY

AUSTRALIA

NETHERLANDS

CANADA

USA

BELGIUM

FRANCE

SWITZERLAND

ITALY

International 0800 is, without doubt, a free service well worth paying for. Prospects may dial in to your number directly without going through the operator. And, incidentally, the 0800 can be connected to a facsimile machine as well as to an ordinary telephone.

International 0800 numbers currently cost £55 a month for the first number and then £27.50 a month for each subsequent number.

Planning and inbound call service

All too often incoming telephone numbers are advertised which create very little appeal or incentive for the prospect to call right away. 'Ring for your brochure' is fine, but a stronger approach would encourage the prospect to action: for example, 'Ring for your brochure before 3 o'clock and we promise to put it in the post to you first class the same day.' Or even 'Ring for your brochure this week: post back a completed booking form to us and we'll arrange to send you a pocket camera or . . .' Why not? It is an accepted fact of direct response that mailing with an incentive will often outpull a straight offer. The same creative planning should be used for incoming call generation.

Testing the incoming call system is rarely undertaken at the moment. But there is no better way of projecting likely response than by testing on a particular conurbation, or approach, so that the amount of likely callers may be realistically assessed and the correct number of telephone lines made available. On the current hit-and-miss attitude of many advertisers, the situation often arises where advertised telephone lines are permanently engaged to the frustration of the caller, and the detriment of the campaign, or a large number of idle manned telephones have been needlessly booked and paid for.

Transcription

Every system has a flaw. Mostly, the flaw is a human being. Transcription is a problem whether the calls are taken 'live' or enquirers are asked to leave their particulars on the computer answering system.

To minimize errors, it is essential that communicators and their supervisors have an adequate knowledge of each town and county. Emphasis must be placed on the essential need for clear handwriting and a firm issue made of the definite requirement for recording postal codes, which are often the main clue to the true location of the enquirer.

Transcription by way of data keyed straight into the computer is equally at risk; and of course the supervisor must always guard against any problems arising by way of faulty disks or tapes which could mean that the information is completely lost.

On-the-spot data preparation is invaluable. It means that a label or a word-processed letter can be generated almost instantaneously, and, subject to the vagaries of the postal system, relevant information can be in the hands of the enquirer with all possible speed.

10

Using the 0898 Callstream service and computerization in telephone marketing

In December 1985, British Telecom issued the first private agreements allowing organizations such as Audiotext to become connected to the Premium Rate Service Network, subsequently renamed 'Callstream'.

This is the system whereby subscribers are charged additional costs. Currently these are 25 pence per minute for off-peak periods and 38 pence per minute for standard and peak times. British Telecom retain part of the income, and Service Providers receive approximately 17.5 pence a minute, less two per cent for prompt settlement.

New customers are further charged £315 per line for each line connected, unless they are lucky or foresighted enough to be located within the local exchange catchment area of parent Callstream exchanges when the cost is a much lesser amount.

The cost of setting-up in-house is quite high. British Telecom require a minimum of ten lines to be ordered in each location, with a commitment of one year.

Once installed, there is a rental charge from £22.55 per line dependent upon distance from the local exchange catchment area of the parent Callstream exchange.

So, you've got the lines installed (and don't expect this to happen overnight. Currently there is an enormous demand for 0898 Callstream in the UK). What about equipment?

At the moment, the availability is very limited. However, many good products are due to come into the marketplace in the near future, and are currently either in the throes of obtaining BT approvals, or are likely to apply shortly.

The main contenders at the moment are Marconi with their Incalls and Keycalls, and Telsis with their Hi-Call and Sixties systems.

Both companies are situated in the south of England. This is not such a coincidence as it sounds, as Geoff Wilson, the managing director of Telsis, was previously employed by Marconi.

Telsis and Marconi both provide Voice Recognition and Voss or 'Grunt' systems. The Marconi Voice Recognition is based on an American package, and provides for responses such as 'Yes', 'No', numbers one to nine, zero and a few other words. Programmes using this system are operated by a banking group, and have been very successful. Audiotext plc and a few other major service providers use the Voice Recognition for competitions, promotions and special offers.

'Grunt' or Voss is rather simpler. This operates on any noise at all down the phone lines. To make use of the system, one can provide callers with a variety of alternatives, and ask them to respond to the one they believe is correct. For example, one could ask callers: 'Which is the capital city of France. Please answer only when you hear the correct response. Is it London? Is it New York? Is it Paris? Is it Rome?' Providing they remain silent after London, New York and Rome – it wouldn't matter if they yelled out 'cauliflowers' or anything else after Paris – the computer would still respond by saying: 'Congratulations, you have chosen the correct answer to the question.'

Case History

MARLBORO

Philip Morris were enthusiastic to try an 0898 telephone marketing promotion, and their agency, The Wight Co., approached Audiotext to put together a unique competition named the 'Million Pound Phone-in', in which callers were invited to answer questions which could lead them to win a Ferrari and other prizes on the way, such as keyrings, lighters, travel bags and so forth.

An average of 16,000 callers a day dialled our 0898 number, all of whom could claim a prize against submission of the requisite number of Marlboro cigarette packet tops. To get through with the maximum number of points, the name "Marlboro" had to be repeated 15 times.

The name and address of each entrant was captured on the tape and then passed to their Handling House for production of a laser letter.

The campaign was so successful that the award of the coveted European Direct Marketing prize was of no surprise.

The advantage of 'Grunt' or Voss is that the software is simpler to organize and handle, and programmes can be quickly put together. Dependent upon the complexity of the Voice Recognition programme, it can otherwise take the programmer a couple of weeks to bring the system up to an acceptable standard. By this I do not mean that Voice Recognition will be working to an infallible 100 per cent standard. Hopefully, it can reach 90 per cent. However, a willing caller can always fool the programme by talking in a muffled manner.

Once the equipment is in situ, you then need to think about a software package to provide the continuous information needed in order to ensure that you have sufficient statistics available to make judgments on the profitability of each programme.

Case History
COCA-COLA

0898 lines can also be effectively answered by 'line' operators as an inbound operation.

Coca-Cola decided to run a competition in this way for 'Diet Coke', and their agency, FKB, approached Audio-text to put together the telephone promotion. 50 operators sat in front of computers which accessed hundreds of questions and answers. Each caller's name and address was captured and a random question was asked, giving the caller an opportunity to answer correctly and enter the prize draw.

Callers obviously enjoyed the novelty of entering this unique competition and a large percentage became eligible for a gift.

Setting up an 0898 is not easy. Neither is it cheap. You have to consider battery back-up in the event of electrical failure, maintenance staff and ancillary equipment in terms of audio cassettes, recording equipment, monitoring devices and programmers.

Probably the best way to enter the marketplace is via a management service using the lines, computers and expertise of an existing service provider.

The fledgling 0898 industry has run into certain problems. For example, in February 1989, British Telecom 'pulled' the lines of the highly publicized *Chatline* services as a result of consumer complaints of excessive telephone bills.

ICSTIS, an independent committee for the supervision of standards of telephone information services, was established in 1986 under the chairmanship of Mr Louis Blom-Cooper QC. Its code of practice on the contents of communications published in 1989 states the following:

ALL SERVICES

1.1 Communications must not contain false, out-of-date or misleading information.

1.2 Communications must not be of a kind that are likely to:
   a encourage or incite any person to commit a criminal offence;
   b cause grave or widespread offence by reason of their sexual or violent content;
   c debase, degrade or demean;
   d induce or promote racial disharmony;
   e encourage, incite or suggest to any person the use of harmful substances;
   f encourage or incite any person to engage in dangerous practices;
   g induce an unacceptable sense of fear or anxiety;
   h result in any unreasonable invasion of privacy;
   i mislead any person with respect to the content or cost of the service being offered;
   j prolong or delay the service unreasonably.

EXPERT OR SPECIALIST SERVICES

2.1 Communications containing information or advice involving the skill and judgment of an expert or specialist, must indicate clearly the identity, current status and any relevant professional qualifications and experience of the person(s) supplying the specialist information or advice at the beginning of the communication.

2.2 Where specialist services contain advice, the communication must be prefaced with a statement that the recipient of the communication should not act upon such advice without first consulting a suitably qualified practitioner in the particular field of the relevant specialism.

2.3 All specialist communications should be conveyed in a manner that properly reflects the seriousness of the subject matter of the advice.

RELGIOUS AND POLITICAL COMMUNICATIONS

3.1 Communications which reflect a particular religious or political viewpoint must paydue regard to the sensibilities of those who may reasonably be expected to hold differing religious beliefs or political opinions.

CHILDREN AND YOUNG PERSONS AND OTHER DEPENDENT PERSONS

4.1 Communications, either wholly or in part, designed for, aimed at or intended for an audience of children and young persons must not include:

a references to sexual practices that a reasonable parent would not wish his or her child to know about;

b language that a reasonable parent would not wish his or her child to hear.

4.2 Communications must not involve any invasion of privacy of any child or young person, or any mentally disordered or mentally handicapped person, or of any other dependent person, having regard to the special protection needed for such dependent persons.

4.3 Communications must not encourage children and young persons, or any other dependent persons, to ring additional telephone numbers.

4.4 Communications aimed at, or intended for an audience of children or young persons should be prefaced by a short statement explaining that the service is more expensive than an ordinary telephone call and should only be used with the agreement of the person responsible for paying the telephone bills.

CHARITIES

5.1 Communications aimed at raising revenue for charitable purposes should be prefaced with a statement identifying the fund raiser, the name of the charity and the charitable object to which the funds are being donated.

For an up-to-date copy of the code write to: The Secretary, ICSTIS, 67–69 Whitfield Street, London W1P 5RL, Tel: 0345 345 005.

Integration of voice and data

Telephone marketing is a modern medium. Technology is improving daily and we are of course only at the very edge of the developments. Incoming call divisions need constantly to enhance productivity in order continually to boost profits. Systems have been developed which allow the communicator to receive an enquiry and immediately retrieve the information sought and have it displayed on a computer screen.

Should the enquirer be, for example, one of the sales reps, it is now quite commonplace to transmit a copy of the information directly to him through a modem.

This is the age of the teleworker. The increased communications efficiency achieved by a company taking full benefits from the technical possibilities more than justifies the outlay, and provides opportunities to move quickly into overseas markets.

Pizzas by phone

Pizzas by phone has evolved into a national business. Very few students or busy families with a penchant for fast food have not heard about the Domino home delivery service. And the same applies to local Chinese take-aways and forward-thinking delicatessens.

Using the telephone makes buying theatre tickets too an extremely attractive and easy operation.

In the USA, the Sears, Roebuck Company has test-marketed a service for paying accounts called Quick Pay. Their credit card customers in Los Angeles are allowed to pay bills by dialling a specific telephone number. Using touch tone MF (multi-frequency) phones they can be connected with operators to give their instructions. Money is then automatically withdrawn from subscribers' accounts at any bank. The subscribers pay a fee of around $4 a month for the service.

Researchers believe that by the end of this century, between 25 and 50 per cent of all payments will be made electronically by telephone.

Customers of forward-thinking banks can now check their balances, transfer monies and pay bills by using portable computer terminals which plug into the telephone.

Not far away is commonly available home shopping. Already the satellite and cable TV companies have entered the field and report that consumers prefer and enjoy entering into transactions in this way.

MF phones will assist in the development of home shopping. These are the telephones which emit a signal, allowing the caller to indicate credit card numbers or anything else simply by pressing the appropriate numbers on the receiver. Unfortunately, only one per cent MF penetration was available in 1988 but the situation is expected to improve rapidly. The forecast for 1993/1994 is 15–18 million.

Data Support

Don't let technology dictate your pace. Before making a major commitment, do involve your communicators in helping to identify those areas of your telephone marketing which could benefit from a data system.

Take into account volume and sources; and how the system will interact with other computers in the company. It could well be that the answers to these questions will prove that currently you may need to 'shelve' the matter of data support until your telephone marketing department begins to grow in terms of numbers of calls to be data-prepped.

Inter-active, voice recognition systems discussed above are expensive animals to buy and to operate. Justification for their purchase has to be call volume. Conversely, smaller systems can prove to be a stop gap only in a growing department, and it is important to be aware of future needs in terms of prospect identification; repeat calling information; list management; de-duplication and reporting.

The primary source data must be built so that priorities and trends can be identified quickly and used as control data to measure costs and performances against a standard.

Telephone marketing managers must identify needs at an early stage so that successful data processing can be successfully integrated to become an effective way to enhance current and future activities.

Computer software for telemarketing

TeleMagic

There are some excellent programmes available, among them the simple-to-use but effective TeleMagic software which comes from 'Remote Control' (514 Via de la Valle, Suite 306, Del Mar, CA 92014, USA). They describe their programme as being suitable for 'people who want to get things done, efficiently, easily, on schedule, at the least possible cost. People who use the phone, write notes, letters, schedule, and follow up a lot, these are the people who will most appreciate Tele-Magic.'

There are of course petty irritations in using an American programme. Not the least is always having to remember to put the date in back-to-front with the month coming first. Then there are the zip instead of post-codes. Having acclimatized oneself to these differences, there is every advantage in using the simple scripting, which assists salespeople by standardizing responses to objections, and providing accurate and swift answers to customer service/support enquiries.

TeleMagic is excellent for inbound as well as outbound enquiries. Three other American manufacturers have pioneered software for telephone marketing. A main area of sales has been the *Fortune* 1000 companies. As an indication of the growth and respect for this medium in the USA, A.T. & T. reports that during 1983 US companies spent $13.6 billion on telephone marketing phone calls and equipment – phones, lines, computers. And *Fortune* estimated telephone sales of goods and services at $75 billion annually. Although figures are not as yet available from BT, I believe that the UK will rapidly follow this trend.

Early, Cloud & Co of Rhode Island has developed state-of-the-art software to support inbound and outbound telephone marketing on any Wang VS equipment. The system has the ability for end-users to create their own telephone marketing scripts and has a high degree of menu response for ease of usage in view of the fact that communicators are unlikely to be trained DP operators. Benefits of computerized software include:

Script control processor. This ensures that communicators never need to pause and wait while conversing with prospects.
Data Formatting. This provides for the possibility of receiving and sending to outside systems for validation.
Dynamic loading. Highlighting key points of campaign ensuring higher sales-closing ratios.
Script builder. Allows non-DP staff the opportunity to generate scripts in a shorter time and provides for communicator to enhance where circumstances allow for this.
Disposition codes. The system maintains all statistical information.
Real time activity monitor. Provides capability to monitor individual operator applications, campaigns and office performance. Aids and quickens supervisory functions.

Datapoint in the UK has evolved some excellent software which has many enthusiastic users in telephone marketing. Many other functions are available in using their system, which (like all systems) does not come cheaply, but certainly covers all features of a successful operation.

Telephone marketing is unique in that it does not simply decrease sales costs, but also increases revenues. The merger of the telephone and data processing technologies is an invaluable tool for achieving success.

11

The winning combination

Telephone marketing can stand on its own merits, but when combined with direct mail, it can in certain circumstances produce really startling results. The trick is to put together a 'winning combination', one which can increase the value of both media, dramatically and cost-effectively.

This chapter tells you how to go about it.

The winning formula works in a variety of situations, but it is most obviously successful in 'cold calls' – especially when these factors are involved:

- the name and address of your file is an unknown quantity;
- your own company is not a household name;
- introducing a brand-new product or service to the market;
- you're unsure which person within your prospect's company is the decision-maker;
- you're offering a high-value product or service for sale;
- the product needs detailed explanation – as, for example, for a piece of technical equipment;
- the product's or service's appeal is limited to certain periods of the year, or depends on contractual or other arrangements; and
- the market is very precisely defined – possibly consisting only of organizations within certain classifications, having specific turnovers, or a particular number of personnel.

If your marketing situation fits any – or several – of these criteria, then a combined direct mail and phonesell operation can be of major help. But which comes first, the chicken or the egg? The telephoning or the direct mail?

The answer to that depends first of all on how accurate your mailing list is, and whether it is made up of larger firms or owner/manager businesses. If the latter is the case – for example, if you have an accurate current list of 25,000 confectioners/ tobacconists/newsagents (CTNs) and you intend to exclude multiples – then the first step in your two-stage campaign might well be a mailing. That's because you can be secure in the knowledge that it will almost certainly be the decision-maker who opens your envelope and reads your mailing piece.

Let's take the case of a well-known confectionery manufac- turer whom we'll call 'Jones'. Each year, that company faces the same problem – that of making sure it has produced enough Easter eggs to meet the anticipated demand but having no stock remaining on its shelves after Easter Monday. The Jones Company needs to create a demand which can be filled by the 500 wholesalers who already stock its merchandise – and it needs to do this in good time if accurate production is to be planned.

It solved its problem in this way:

An attractive 'pop-up' mailing piece was sent out in the second week of January. This offered the 25,000 CTNs (i) an incentive in the form of an opportunity to enter an exciting holiday competition when they placed an order for the Jones Easter eggs and (ii) attractive mobile window display materials.

A covering letter contained a list of the wholesalers stocking the product, categorized by area, and asked the CTN to phone- in if his own particular supplier was not on this list. All direct accounts were excluded from this promotion and eliminated from the mailing.

Research showed that the Jones Company's mailing piece – packaged attractively and detailing the Incentive Holiday Scheme – was received enthusiastically by the CTN retailers. Moreover 1381 CTNs telephoned to say their usual wholesalers were not on Jones's list. This information gave Jones's sales force the opportunity to visit those wholesalers and convert them into customers, by *proving* that a real demand for Jones's Easter eggs existed in the retail trade.

By 1 February 3,612 CTNs had entered Jones's holiday competition – proving they had actually placed orders with their wholesalers. These 3,612, together with the 1,381 who had made incoming calls, were then eliminated from the master promo- tional file; the rest were telephoned over a two-week period, using the script shown in Figure 12.

Figure 12 Sample script

Introduction
Good morning/afternoon, my name is . . . , and I'm calling on behalf
of Jones's Confectionery Co. Are you the owner or manager, sir/
madam?

(Owner/Manager)

May I have your name please? _____

With only a few weeks before the Easter egg rush, we want to make
sure you acted on the mailing piece we sent a couple of weeks ago.
You do remember the leaflet with the pop-up, don't you
Mr/Mrs. . . . ?   yes/no

a   *If yes*:
Have you placed your order yet for Jones's Bunny Easter egg, Mr/
Mrs. . . . ?   yes/no

b   *If no*:
The Jones range of Easter eggs is going to be very heavily advertised
on TV, Mr/Mrs. . . . Retail prices range from 50p to £5 and each egg is
colourfully packaged with attractive red and blue ribbons, and the
more expensive have satin-lined boxes. The hollow eggs are a new
recipe milk chocolate and the filled eggs contain our best-selling
Golden Assortment. If you give me the name of your usual distributor,
Mr/Mrs. . . . , I will make sure he has sufficient stock, or else I will call
you back with the name of your nearest stockist. Who is your usual
wholesaler, Mr/Mrs. . . . ?

What sort of price range do you usually buy? The smaller eggs are in
outers of 12 and the larger ones are in cartons of 3s.

_____ outers of 12
_____ outers of 3

Objection	*Response*
Already placed order for other products/I've spent too much/Easter egg business is declining	I do recommend you include Bunnies in your stock. We have two-minute spot ads in peak viewing times and this always makes demand heavy. We can also arrange attractive window and counter display material.
I'd like to see what they look like.	I'll put another leaflet in the post to you today, Mr/Mrs. . . . Thank for time, etc.

This promotion produced an immediate response of a further 712 definite orders. This meant not only a successful launch of the product, but a total sell-out for the manufacturer.

When the telephone call is the first stage

The Easter egg promotion is an example of one in which the mailing pieces should *precede* the telephone call.

But, however good your file of prospect names and addresses may be, there are many instances when the telephone call should cost-effectively precede the mailing, instead of the other way around.

Take the case of a timeshare operation. Here, the company produced a very colourful brochure and attendant literature, which cost approximately £1.50, posted to a UK address. Media coupon advertising had brought in a very fair response, but conversions following the mailing out of the information package continued to be low.

A telephone questionnaire was undertaken. This showed that while the content of the package was attractive, the respondents to the coupon advertising campaign were, in the main, not really prospective timeshare buyers for a variety of reasons, such as age, holiday requirements, numbers in the family, and so forth.

Before proceeding to mail out any more brochures, the company organized a telephone follow-up call to those prospects who had sent in coupons. Each was thanked for having expressed interest, and gently probed to see if they could be converted into becoming subscribers to the scheme. Of those sending in coupons 23 per cent were discounted in this way, at a saving of £1.50 per name and address. Of the remainder, 40 per cent responded with further interest when the courteous call was followed up by the company's informative, albeit expensive, mailing piece.

My company has used the same two-stage technique cost-effectively for a wide variety of merchandise and services. One case involved a developer and his agent who were trying to rent out shops in a new precinct. They were spending considerable sums of money on advertising the available space in the press, on TV and radio, via direct mail. Due to various factors, the shops moved very slowly and the leases became a serious problem.

The developer produced a list of his ideal tenants, covering every kind of retail outlet, as well as ancillary services such as cleaners, shoe repairers, launderettes, and so forth.

A telephone call was made to every outlet of these types in a radius of two miles of the shopping precinct. The object was to speak to the decision-maker (and, in the case of multiples, to find out the names and addresses of people in authority) to determine whether there was possible interest in the leases being offered.

Of those contacted 11 per cent indicated that they might consider a shop in the new precinct, and each of these was mailed a brochure and a personalized letter. This gave details of viewing times, rents, length of leases being offered, and all other relevant information.

Of the people who were mailed this material 40 per cent later actually contacted the developer's agents. 229 viewed the property and a sizeable number of the leases were disposed of, at an overall cost to the developer of just £6,000.

Another example of the same formula concerns a large paper group which wished to introduce into the marketplace a new hand-drying machine using their own paper products.

An excellent sales force had tried repeatedly to make inroads into larger industrial and commercial premises, but without much success. The main stumbling block was that it proved very difficult to pinpoint who was the individual company's decision-maker responsible for purchasing washroom equipment, and even more difficult to contact the person who could influence such an order.

Media advertising and direct mail brought insufficient response to provide enough 'leads' and it was therefore decided to telephone 11,000 companies who fitted certain parameters, such as size. The companies were told the purpose of the call and the questionnaire looked like the one shown in Figure 13.

It was found, in the main, that the switchboard operators of the contacted companies were able and willing to provide the necessary answers; as a result, 8,700 questionnaires were fully completed. One interesting and important fact which emerged was that it was the managing director's *personal secretary* who often was the most influential in making such decisions.

Figure 13 Questionnaire

Name of company _____ Head office _____ No. of staff in building _____
Address _____ Tel ____
No. of toilets:
Male _____ Female _____
Purchasing officer(s) _____
(1) Current hand-drying methods _____
(2) Are they satisfactory? _____
Executive director _____
Managing director's PA/Secretary _____
Personnel Welfare Officer _____

A personalized mailing was then sent to the 23,000 individual names and addresses at the 8,700 firms. Salesmen were given copies of the letters, together with the information sheets, and they were then able to visit every outlet, knowing who would influence such a decision, what the opposition was – and if equipment currently in use was satisfactory.

This promotion helped to successfully launch the product.

Phone-mail-phone combinations

In 25 years in direct mail marketing, the question I have been asked most frequently is, 'What is the *minimum* response I can expect from my mailing campaign?'

It is a question which is impossible to answer, because it depends on so many factors such as lists, mailing pieces, timing, pricing, appeal and, of course, the need for the product or service being offered. Yet a three-stage approach can guarantee a success rate because of the very nature of the promotion itself. Here's how it works:

Stage 1

The initial telephone call confirms company particulars, the number of employees or whatever else is relevant. It also obtains the name – and often the ear – of the decision-maker, so as to introduce the product or service and get agreement to be sent the relevant literature.

Stage 2

A personalized letter and accompanying literature is then sent out by first class post to those whose reactions were positive, advising them to expect a second telephone call either in order to sell to them directly or to make an appointment for a sales person to call.

Stage 3

The 'clincher call' comes from four to six days after mailing.

These three-stage promotions have been used very widely for a variety of organizations, including:

Computer software and hardware
Car leasing
Business travel
Courier services
Equipment of every kind
Machine tools
Advertising space selling
Advertising and PR services
Accounting management
Office cleaning
Hiring
Credit collection
Insurance.

In each case, the prospect list has been clearly defined by the first call, and the name of the decision-maker pinpointed. Whenever the company proves not to be a realistic prospect, its name and address is removed from the list. In the second, or personalized mailing stage, material is posted only to the 'positives' on the list, and when the third stage comes around, the prospect is conversant with the company's services or products and therefore more likely to agree to buy or to see a representative.

The same three-stage technique can be used successfully in consumer promotions.

Figure 14 Sample script

First telephone call (preceding mailing)

1   Good evening Mr/Mrs. . . . , My name is Mary of the XYZ Painting Company. We are the people who guarantee our outside painting for 25 years. Has your house been painted within the last year, Mr/Mrs. . . . ?   (yes/no)
a   *If yes*: May I send you some literature for future reference then, Mr/Mrs. . . . ?   (yes/no)
b   *If no*: Do you normally have your house painted regularly, Mr/Mrs. . . . ? After all, we all have to protect one of the largest investments we ever make in buying a house, don't we? Is yours a 2/3/4-bedroomed house, Mr/Mrs. . . . ? (pause for comment)

2   I would like to send you some literature and then phone you back after you've had a chance to look at it, Mr/Mrs. . . . Which day would suit you best? (M/Tu/W/Th/F/S) (am/pm)
And which time?

Second telephone call (following mailing)

1   Good evening, Mr/Mrs. . . . This is Mary of XYZ Painting. I'm phoning you as promised. Did you receive our literature?
   Our Mr Jones is in your area for the next two weeks. He would like to call on you and discuss the substantial savings that can be made by using XYZ. Are you free on a Monday evening or would you prefer another day or time? (M/Tu/W/Th/F/S) (am/pm)

Objection	Answer
Can't afford to have my house painted.	XYZ is really inexpensive and is guaranteed for 25 years.
Have to know cost before I allow salesman to come along.	I wish I could tell you, but this does vary considerably. All I do know is that you will save money.
Only had house painted two years ago.	How long will it last though, Mr/Mrs. . . . ? Now is the time to look at XYZ before prices rise again.
Thinking of moving.	Then you're just the person to use XYZ, Mr/Mrs. . . . It will without doubt enhance the value of your house.

For example, let us look at a company which offers a long-term outside house painting scheme. By its very nature, its services are expensive, and experience showed the company that it could only expect *houseowners* to be interested in making use of such a service – and not short-term leaseholders who are unlikely to invest money in maintaining a landlord's property.

One of the most difficult things to ask a stranger is, 'Do you own your own house?' All too often, the reply – if there is any at all – is along the lines of 'Mind your own business'. The phonesell script in this instance therefore had to be particularly soft-sell and the communicators needed to read very carefully. There are more ways than one, however, of skinning a cat, and question 1 in the script (Figure 14) was carefully designed to eliminate those who were not house-owners, and therefore had no investment to protect.

The subsequent mailing letter was, again, personalized and began by thanking the prospect for his or her time on the telephone, and ended by referring to the fact that a second telephone call would be made in a few days' time.

The personal approach

Direct mail copy, when it is used to follow a telephone call, should be devoid of gimmicks for two important reasons. One is that the prospect has already had the initial discussion and has expressed an interest; he or she will therefore expect to receive the fullest possible details rather than just an 'appetite whetter'.

The other reason is more mundane – the more you spend on the gimmick, the less profitable your campaign becomes. There is a lot of controversy between a short three-and-a-half paragraph message and a two-page letter. Providing, however, that the advantages to the recipient, rather than to the sender, are clearly indicated in the opening paragraphs, and providing that motivation for action is incorporated at the end or in a postscript, I have never found length to be an important factor in response levels.

If the mailing list is on tape, then laser techniques can be used to provide inexpensive personalized letters and contents. At time of writing, this can be done for as little as 14 pence each.

However, the laser industry is in its infancy and it may well be
that the price will have altered considerably when this book
appears in print.

Alternative personalization is readily and competitively available by use of word processors and auto-typewriters. Where
large quantities are needed but the budget is low, a printed letter
can be matched with a typed address, using a carbon ribbon
typewriter.

The letter should of course be personalized as much as
possible, using the various factors which were learned in the first
stage telephone call. These personal factors are underlined in
the sample letter shown in Figure 15.

Figure 15 Appointment letter

The XYZ 25-Year Guaranteed Painting Company

Date _____

Mr J. Brown
211 Courtenay Crescent
Glasgow GL1 4TB

Dear Mr Brown,
Thank you for talking to me on the telephone on Wednesday evening.
I did enjoy our chat and, as promised, enclose details of the XYZ 25-
year painting plan which is guaranteed to save you a
great deal of money on a 3-bedroomed house like
yours.

As you usually have your house painted every five years, the XYZ
(which is probably only slightly more exensive than the old-fashioned
method) it will save you the price of four coats. Bearing in mind the
rate of inflation, you will be £s in pocket, and I have no doubt you
must agree that the finish of an XYZ painted house is really superior
and stands out from its neighbours.

As you asked, I will call you personally on Tuesday evening
between 7.30 and 8.00 p.m. If this is not convenient, please don't
hesitate to call my office which will gladly arrange another time.

I do look forward to speaking with you again and hearing your
comments on the literature I've enclosed with this letter.
Yours sincerely
Mary Green

P.S. If we can fix up an appointment before the end of February, we
can offer you a 10% discount if you decide to place an order.

An important point to remember – yet often forgotten – is to eliminate those who spontaneously respond verbally or in writing after receiving the second stage mailer. Calling them as if they had not done so is irritating to the prospect and, of course, needlessly expensive.

Test the different methods

As in all direct marketing, it is as well to take a small bite of the apple before you swallow a whole fruit which might possibly have a worm hidden inside it. A test of 1,000 names and addresses for the XYZ Company could look like this:

	Total	Cost	No. of orders	Cost per order
Mailing 'cold'	250	£100	2	£ 50
Telephoning 'cold'	250	£250	2.5	£100
Telephone and mail follow-up	250	£350	9	£ 39
Three-stage	250	£600	20	£ 30

While a company would deduce that a 'cold' mailing could be more cost-effective than 'cold' telephoning, it is evident that a two-stage combination increases results, while a three-stage promotion, involving perhaps mailing only 100 of the original 250 telephoned, would prove the most cost-effective method of all.

If, however, you are a video company selling a 'name' video tape to retail stockists, then the same test package could produce entirely different results.

	Total	Cost	No. of tapes sold	Cost per order
Mailing 'cold'	250	£100	40	£2.50
Telephoning 'cold'	250	£250	100	£2.50
Mail and telephone	250	£350	135	£2.60

In this instance, there would be little point in launching a three-stage approach. The video tape distributor would be well advised either to 'cold call' directly by telephone, or to

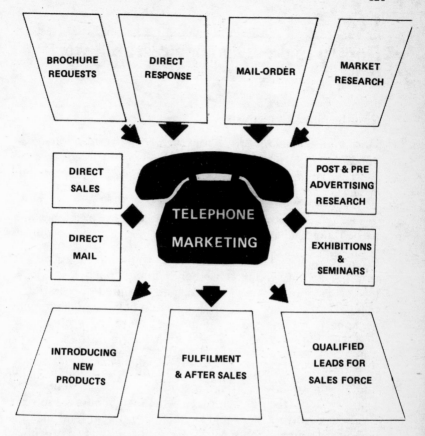

undertake a two-stage promotion – first, by mailing full information, order forms and reply paid envelope, and then following through with a telephone call to the non-respondents.

Telephone and direct mail prove an ideal combination everywhere – and one which is always flexible, speedy, and cost-effective.

12

How to make telephone research work harder

by John Orsmond

The author, John Orsmond, is chairman of Advertising Research Marketing Ltd. Established in 1979, the company is in the top ten per cent of the UK's full-service marketing communications agencies.

'In my experience, the best decisions are always taken by the men with
the best information.'   Disraeli

What Disraeli said of politics is just as true for business people working in commercial, consumer and industrial fields. Today, businesses of every kind and size are confronted by a bewildering array of technologies, all designed to help them gather and evaluate more information than ever before. How effectively that information is then used can often determine the success or failure of a project.

The aim of this chapter is to focus attention on the commercial application of information. Specifically, it outlines how the combination of the right approach with the right information can be used to solve a sales and marketing problem, and make a significant contribution towards the profitability of an organization. The case study detailed later in this chapter describes why telephone techniques were chosen and how they were used.

Information gathering

In our experience across many markets, we have found a widespread incidence of bad research habits. These include: setting up research programmes on a very narrow base; depending on intermittent ad hoc studies which produce isolated results; frequently resorting to the smallest sample sizes and using the cheapest research methods; using research to support decisions already taken or programmes already in place.

But, by using research as an integral part of an overall sales and marketing strategy, we have found that it can bring a unique value to your business picture.

Broadly speaking, you can conduct either qualitative or quantitative research, entailing the use of fieldwork, postal, or telephone techniques. The trick is to know whether to use just one of these techniques – or a combination. And more especially, when and how to use them in conjunction with other marketing communications activities.

Telephone methods

Consistent with the huge growth in communications, a growing number of applications are being developed for the telephone.

In the main, applications have largely been connected to the selling line – the most visible of areas. Consequently, over recent years we have seen the rise of tele-sales departments within organizations as well as an increasing number of bureaux offering inbound/outbound services.

As is usually the case, it has been the big-volume FMOG markets which have created the greatest demand for these services. However, commercial and industrial companies are also becoming more sophisticated in vertical market strategies, and are now developing more effective telephone techniques to drive programmes such as seminars, road-shows and the like.

Otherwise, where the telephone has been used in information-gathering exercises, we have found it is most often restricted to lead qualification. While this somewhat 'narrow' use of the telephone is of vital importance in boosting sales representatives' call ratios, it still falls short of deploying telephone techniques to their full.

There is a better and far more effective way.

Those companies exercising a breadth of vision – by integrating research into their marketing strategy– have already tapped into the secret. But as general levels of interest grow, their hard-won and presently closely-guarded lessons will become more readily available – helping a new generation of sales and marketing professionals to find improved methods of working.

Best choice – the winning combination

My experience indicates that when you adopt a balanced marketing communications strategy, telephone techniques play a vital role. They can be used to perform specific tasks which no other research technique can fulfil, and to drive general sales and marketing programmes more cost-effectively than other techniques allow.

Our case studies indicate that the combination of telephone research techniques and direct marketing is one of the most powerful marriages; helping you to achieve the most desirable of unions – the growth of turnover as well as profitability.

As a guideline, the most effective formula for bringing these two disciplines together is:

i	Background:	Research
		Telephone
		Reporting and evaluation
ii	Preparatory:	Specification
		Planning
		Budgeting
		Materials origination
		Team formation
		Telephone testing
		Materials production
iii	Implementation:	Direct marketing
		Telephone follow-up
		Appointments
iv	Evaluation:	Performance tracking and reporting
		Programme refinement
		Next-stage forward planning

These stages require methodical consideration and usually, more time than is generally understood. However, in what is a complex combination of variables, it is worth avoiding the temptation to proceed in ignorance for the sake of speed. Allow more time in order to work to the highest professional standards possible. Shortcuts often lead to short change.

Sourcing – forming the right team

No matter how thoroughly the above stages are prepared and implemented, the quality of the people you employ or choose to work with will prove to be your strongest – or weakest – link in the chain.

Teamwork is of the essence, whether choosing to develop fully-fledged internal resources, or seeking total package external sources.

Internal resources

Setting up and developing an internal department is well covered elsewhere in this book – and outlines the needs for employing (and firing), housing, equipping and training. My working experience across a wide variety of clients suggests that internal resourcing requires very careful consideration, with a detailed understanding of the long-term commitment involved. Remember – it is inadvisable to set your foot on the first rung without first knowing the length of the ladder.

External resources

Opting for the right external source offers you a number of distinctive benefits. Suppliers who can demonstrate proven professional standards will virtually eliminate your needs for training, and speed of throughput should be higher from the start. This option also provides you with great flexibility – enabling you to deploy techniques intensively at certain times of the year. This 'tap on/tap off' flexibility is particularly suitable should you be working in markets with pronounced seasonal/cyclical peaks and troughs, but it also increases demands on you to deliver the fullest-possible briefings. Details kept close to your chest can often be your own undoing.

Choosing the external suppliers who are to form a part of your team poses the usual challenges. It is as well to be reminded of the basic tenets:

Who are they?
Who uses them?
What work have they done?
Where are they located?

What is their size?

How broad or specialist are their capabilities?

And last, but not least, how experienced are they in forming accurate working budgets on a fixed package basis (allowing for variables such as BTUs and helping you to avoid any 'hidden extras')?

Any bona fide professional should put their know-how at your disposal, helping you to arrive at fully detailed specifications as well as associated costs.

Generally, you are likely to be confronted by two schools of practice in this respect. On the one hand, there are those consultants or agencies who may ask for a commitment fee to form the working proposals and budgets. And, on the other, there are those who consider the formation of working proposals and budgets as a part of the initial development stages – and will do so without fees, or at a nominal commitment charge. Broadly, I believe clients realize the best value when working on a time fee + cost of project basis.

Another hallmark of the professionals is that they can offer you understanding – both of the immediate requirement and in helping you formulate a longer-range view.

A good professional will have also ensured that pre-testing has eradicated most pitfalls, enabling you to pursue continual improvement in your future research activities. In my experience, the growth of learning and experience works best in a relationship where there is free exchange of information on all sides. Therefore, last and probably most important, our golden rule is to work with people who have integrity and are like-minded.

Case study

To adapt a famous definition, research is: using the right method to gather the right information from the right places at the right time for the right price.

Marking communications may be defined as: using the right media to convey the right information to the right places at the right time for the right price.

As this case study indicates, by combining these two approaches, excellent results may be anticipated.

The starting point for any well-run project begins by considering your business circumstance relative to the marketplace. Our inclination is to avoid the tendency of focusing too much attention on competitors. After all, the goal of an exercise is not to end up doing business with your competitors!

The client I have chosen for this case study is a subsidiary of one of the world's largest light-metal manufacturers and has an established UK trading performance of more than 30 years. Their product range serves three major market segments in the agricultural, retail and consumer fields. Their largest traditional business base has been in the agricultural area, leaving the other two areas to 'look after themselves'. However, with changes in EC legislation beginning to hamper their order intake in the agricultural area, there was an urgent need to restore business development in the other two existing markets.

My company's involvement on behalf of the client began by building a very broad picture, focusing effort on the areas of greatest potential. In other words, implementing 'least effort-largest yield' programmes.

The initial stages then, were devoted to gaining understanding so that the feasibility of a full-blown research programme could be tested, and consequent programmes could be designed with insight. The early stages of work revealed what we have found to be one of the most common oversights in companies of every kind and size: there had been little or no quantifiable analysis of their most valuable resource – their customers.

Putting customers first

Therefore, the first step was to undertake a detailed analysis of sales for both the consumer and retail areas. Briefly, these studies were based on the previous three years of trading and focused on:

i   The territories from which the others had come
ii   The value bands of the orders
iii   When the orders were made in each calendar year.

Working with the client, these broad measures enabled us to

see the big numbers first. We could then direct more detailed enquiries which enabled us to find out what had been done in each of the three years to achieve the results. We find that these simple disciplines are all too often neglected.

Putting prospects next

Our preliminary work then turned attention to the marketplace with a view to defining its value, size i.e. number of establishments, and geographical distribution. It is vital to gain a statistical appreciation of these measures in order to assess your ability to match the scale of the project. (In this case, the field sales force numbered three – with two internal sales staff.)

Our initial marketplace evaluation revealed that there were very few readily available detailed reports of the UK marketplace. However, it did disclose the number and calibre of list sources available. From these, it was possible to arrive at the market size which numbered some 1,500 establishments. These were of mixed kind, with concentrations of around 40 per cent in the south, 22 per cent in the Midlands, and 26 per cent in the north (See Table 1). There was little bunching of the establishments in each of those regions. Plainly, the specification of the project would have to take this into account, to ensure that the client's sales force was not overstretched.

The findings of the Sales and Market reports were then correlated and the following major conclusions noted:

i   The client's three-year sale pattern almost identically matched the market shape with 37 per cent in the south, 25 per cent in the Midlands, and 24 per cent in the north (see Table 2).

ii Some 60 per cent of the order values lay between the bands of £9,000 and £30,000 with the highest concentration towards the upper end.

iii There was some cyclical effect with downturns around spring and an upturn towards September/October.

There was clearly very strong potential for our client, and on this basis the project specification was taken to its working stage and budgets.

Our in-house facilities were used to form a computerised

database suitable for both the research, and later the direct marketing stages. Concurrently, it was necessary to decide the method of reaching the marketplace. It is of critical importance at this stage to decide whether or not you require 100 per cent penetration of the marketplace, or can work with smaller sampling techniques. In this instance, it was necessary to achieve a 100 per cent coverage. Given the total size of the marketplace (1,500 establishments) we selected telephone techniques to ensure a 100 per cent coverage – and return.

In our experience, telephone techniques are unrivalled in this respect.

The questionnaire

The earlier working stages had fully revealed how little was known. Therefore, it was possible to design the questionnaire with very specific requirements in mind. Broadly, the questionnaire covered the following main areas:

Profile – by kind, size and location of establishment
Materials – by kind of building materials used in the past and preferred
Timing – by order cycles and building cycles
Ranking – by what attributes they considered to be most suitable or desirable
Market awareness – by ranking of known suppliers.

Construction and writing of research questionnaires for telephone techniques should not be left to amateurs. Equally, it is our experience that when forming the questionnaire it is best to consult with the telephone agency you may have selected. Their experience can often prove invaluable in eliminating any difficulties the script may give operators. We have found that consultation at this stage also helps to prime the telephone agency, ensuring that their operators work with confidence. However, while we always ensure that this is done, we also conduct some preliminary testing ourselves, to make certain that our terminology is understood by the people who really matter – the potential customers. Our sourcing for the telephone work in this instance was with Audiotext, the company of which Pauline Marks is Chairman. (Our original connections with Pauline

Marks go back a decade to when we were a small company starting out and required a telephone answering service.)

Conducting the research

Having negotiated a satisfactory arrangement with Audiotext, the questionnaires were then finalized and produced, using the database programme to output and attach self-adhesive address labels directly to the questionnaires. The interviews took place over a period of eight working days. Results were despatched back to us for validation and input to the research database. In this way, it was possible to provide our client with an almost day-to-day snapshot of the crude results.

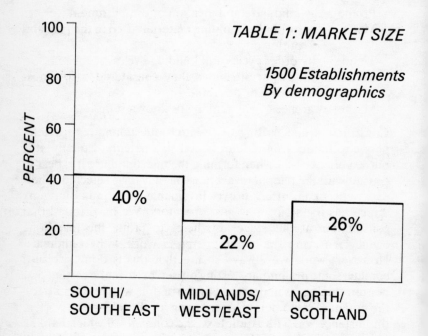

TABLE 1: MARKET SIZE

1500 Establishments
By demographics

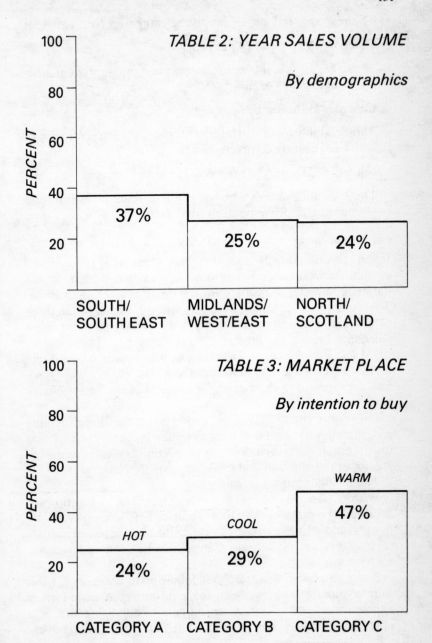

TABLE 2: YEAR SALES VOLUME

By demographics

TABLE 3: MARKET PLACE

By intention to buy

The response fell largely into three categories (see Table 3):

Category A (around 24 per cent)

Those establishments immediately planning improvements – either extensions or new buildings

Category B (around 29 per cent)

Those establishments who had no plans for improvement or who had recently completed work

Category C (around 47 per cent)

Those establishments who had no immediate plans but were considering improvements at some future date

Direct marketing

Upon completion of the telephone research these three categories were coded and new information added to the database in order to prepare for the direct marketing exercise. This comprised personalized letters styled for each of the three categories. The approach was kept extremely simple, using a customized letter and product range information. There was no 'hard sell' in the content. In our view, the purpose of the direct marketing exercise was to inform the recipients in a way which was appropriate to their need. The results of the exercise have since supported that view.

Given our client's small personnel base, the direct mailing programme was phased at a regular quantity per week enabling the internal staff to follow up with courtesy calls, ensuring receipt of information and qualifying possible interest.

The results were staggering.

Within Category A, a five-in-six appointments ratio was achieved! To make certain that the three field sales representatives would achieve 100 per cent call-rate, the internal staff regulated future mailings of Category A by sending fewer out each week.

It was also found that telephone follow-up to Category C (who were considering improvements in the future), resulted in further appointments – but not of any urgency – allowing the field operatives to make 'filler calls' en route to the next prime buyer.

Category B, those who had no need or who had recently completed projects, were also followed up. The appointments ratio here was very low. Nonetheless, the response to the telephone follow-up calls was very positive – helping our client to build good future customer relations.

The bottom line

In our experience, the keynote to achieving successful results is simplicity of execution supported by extremely thorough preparation.

In this case, the winning combination comprised teamwork between all parties – the client, ourselves, and the tele-market agency. Altogether, the specification of the programme comprised:

Initial customer and market research;
Database research and database formation and use;
Questionnaire and telephone research stages;
Direct marketing stages;
Very detailed market research study arising from information gathered.

For the future, and in the absence of published data in the public domain, this research will prove to be a seminal study for this particular market – giving our client an unrivalled information resource for both sales and long-term marketing and communications strategies.

Far more immediate, however, is the bottom line.

The total package cost to the client for all the above stages, including BTUs, was a cost of £11,267. Against this cost, our client won orders worth £224,000 in the first month alone (a cost-to-sale ratio of five per cent which has since fallen as order levels have been sustained). In all the previous years of trading in this particular market segment, their best ever month had realized £91,000.

Success within your reach

Without the telephone, we could not have attempted to produce a piece of research that had so much impact on our client's business picture. We would not have been able to review the marketplace as quickly as we did, nor would we have been able to test the questionnaire as rapidly. Nor could we have achieved 100 per cent penetration and coverage of the marketplace within eight working days. Nor would the client have been able to follow up the information despatched to their prospective customers. Nor could we have kept the sales force out on the road, calling only on those establishments who had a high-priority need to find a good supplier.

Quite simply, the telephone made a vital contribution towards putting higher turnover within our client's reach.

It's within your reach too.

13

Telephone marketing in Europe

165 million telephones were actually in situ in European homes and offices in 1986. In the UK alone, 1988 showed 18 million domestic and five million business installations. By 1992, and the creation of a single market, it is expected that the installed base will increase to an excess of 200 million.

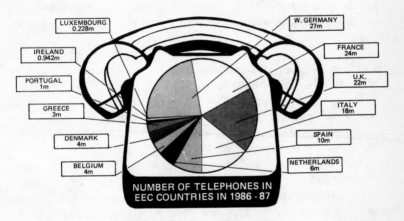

LUXEMBOURG 0.228m
IRELAND 0.942m
PORTUGAL 1m
GREECE 3m
DENMARK 4m
BELGIUM 4m
W. GERMANY 27m
FRANCE 24m
U.K. 22m
ITALY 18m
SPAIN 10m
NETHERLANDS 6m

NUMBER OF TELEPHONES IN EEC COUNTRIES IN 1986 - 87

As competition within the community grows, so telephone marketing will become even more important, with every company vying for a slice of the new cake – but many lacking the financial resources to open up local sales offices.

Germany

Germany and France lead the tables with the largest number of installations. Gunter Greff, a leading expert in telemarketing in Germany and managing director of TAS Telemarketing GmbH as well as co-editor of *Direktmarketing mit neuen Medien*, writes the following: 'Since the 1980s there has been a considerable increase of telephone marketing in Germany, due without doubt to the high cost of sales and the need to compete in a fierce marketplace.

Closely connected with this increase in telephone marketing is the commonplace distribution of computer technology. More and more companies, small as well as large, now install electronic customer files – emphasizing the importance between the telephone and data base marketing.

The legislative situation in Germany

Regrettably German bureaux are only allowed to dial prospects if they are:

a) active existing customers
b) they have previously requested information in writing, by, perhaps, filling in and sending off a coupon from an advertisement.

Legislation prohibits telephone marketing by companies such as wine merchants or newsagents.

Business-to-business calling does not fare much better than telephone marketing approaches to the private sector. Again one can only dial a prospect who has a direct connection to the business of the company who is calling.

Individual cases vary. As an example, the automobile manufacturer, BMW, was prohibited from making telephone marketing calls, because they had contacted professional people inviting them to road test new models. The judge of the OLG (Oberlandesgericht) stated that, in his opinion, this was an unreasonable molestation.

In Germany, there are very strong legal rulings which originate in rule UBG1 (rule against unfair competition).

Service agencies in Germany

There are almost 200 telephone marketing agencies in the country. Many are small (one–five telephone work places) and produce poor or ineffective work. The larger agencies belong to the Fachgruppe Telemarketing in DDV (German Direct Marketing Association) which insists that its members follow the guidelines laid down.

At time of writing the largest agencies in German are TAS Telemarketing with 258 telephone work places, DTM in

Offenbach with around 80 work places and Frey und Linkenheil in Karlsruhe with approximately 60 work places.

Most of the large agencies offer both outbound and inbound telemarketing.

As in every other country, there are large differences between agencies; and I always recommend that prospective clients should seek references and take the time to fully investigate before placing their business.

Organization of in-house departments

More and more companies are installing their own telephone marketing departments. Kodak AG, for example, transact more than 70 per cent of their film business by phone.

All EDV producers have their own teams. In connection with their catalogues, the total EDV accessories are sold in this way. At the same time, where the prospect is a particularly large one, appointments are made for field sales and field service.

DEL computers only sell their PCs by direct marketing – in exactly the same way as they do in the USA.

Telephone marketing statistics in Germany

Estimated number of telemarketing agencies approximately 200

Estimated turn-over volume of agencies   approximately 180 million DM

Estimated turn-over of in-house telemarketing   approximately 700 million DM

Trends

The expansion of telemarketing in Germany, especially of inbound, will undoubtedly increase.

- New applications are on the horizon; home shopping, for example.
- Computer-supported telephone marketing will take the place of manual clerical assistance.
- Europe 1992 will change the qualification profile. We will without doubt need to engage polyglot telemarketeers.

In Germany the growth of the industry is apparent. As one market in 1992, the legal requirements will doubtless change for the benefit of all. However, I believe that it is necessary to ensure the elimination of negative implications such as too much aggressive selling, molestation and annoyance during the late evening hours.

Operating in the correct, controlled manner, will be a decisive factor in the future growth of the industry as a whole.

France

In France alone, there are 150 telephone marketing agencies and a further 300 marketing organizations with telephone resources available to their clients.

Le Syndicat du Marketing Téléphonique in Paris state that 380Ffr million revenue was received by member companies in 1987, and 443Ffr million in 1988 with a 30 per cent increase forecast for 1989. The society estimates 3,500–6,000 orders daily taken by telephone. They list the 25 premier telephone marketing member companies:

Agency	Tel. no	Established
Phone Marketing Systems	45 54 95 96	1979
Téléperformance	48 28 40 30	1978
Actiphone France	47 30 28 28	1980
Phonepermanence	40 59 92 92	1985
Groupe Téléscore	46 71 77 07	1982
Bernard Julhiet Télé-Action	47 96 48 85	1974
Télémedia	42 01 01 01	1983
Téléresources	43 47 31 13	1983
GMSA	47 08 29 29	1981
DPV	45 41 52 02	1977
Sophie de Menthon		
Conseil Gpe Multiligne	45 44 62 71	1976
H2A Télémarketing	40 12 40 10	1987
Interlignes Bayard Presse	47 23 72 92	1979
CALL	48 87 24 00	1983
Médiatel	47 66 04 08	1979

Agency	Tel. no	Established
Phone Communication	45 84 00 10	1985
Prise Directe	46 38 99 99	1986
MV2 Maxiphone	42 53 20 20	1986
Phone Intervention	89 66 28 88	1983
Téléobjectif	48 25 08 08	1984
Actel J.T.C.	39 52 34 21	1980
Phone Impact	47 70 92 92	1982
Maxitel S.A.	45 29 13 31	1984
Stratel	43 56 32 54	1987
Phonix	45 22 20 00	1982

14

Twenty-five ways to make the most of your phone

I'm going to try the impossible in this chapter. I'm going to endeavour to list the endless benefits which a professionally-run and well-controlled telephone campaign can provide to just about every kind of organization under the sun – whether it's big business, a political party, a small-town one-man enterprise, a charity, or 'you name it'.

Because the list is 'endless', because any book has space limitations, and because I trust the reader's intelligence to find new and creative ways in which he or she can apply the techniques described in these pages to his or her organization, I'm ending my list arbitrarily after putting down 25 uses for Alexander Graham Bell's magic management tool.

Like your car, the telephone will take you anywhere you want to go. You've just got to learn to drive and point it in the right direction.

Advanced technological developments – such as the overlay network for the City of London with national and international connections – are making the telephone even more important and useful to every business – indeed, essential to any business wishing to keep ahead in today's tough, competitive climate. These new developments are wonderfully exciting; a great future is in store for us all in the field of telecommunications. Every year – almost every month – brings changes and new developments, even in 'tradition-bound Britain'. The stops are out and the field is wide open, both to the inventive engineer and to British Telecom's competitors.

So, what does the year 2001 hold for us in this respect? And how far have we travelled?

The history of the telephone is rather short, making its rapid development all the more amazing, though these developments have accelerated incredibly within just the past decade or so, thanks to the 'new technology'.

In the very beginning, the user was offered only a very simple system. All calls were directed through the local operator (who became a very popular lady due to her ability to pass on gossip, acquired when she 'forgot' to disconnect from the calls).

Within four years of Alexander Graham Bell's invention, the first patent for automatic switching was granted and the first public telephone exchange began operating, installed in Coleman Street, London, with a total of just eight subscribers.

The genius of Thomas Edison showed itself at this time, and he invented the switchboard.

Although automatic 'switching' was known and indeed actually was in use in Coatbridge, Scotland, in 1886, the British Post Office was in no great hurry to replace the manual arm operator system – despite the fact that more than 20 automatic switching exchanges had been installed in the USA before the year 1900. It was two years before the start of the First World War, in 1912, that the first automatic public telephone exchange in Britain was opened in Epsom, Surrey, with a capacity for serving 500 subscribers.

Here matters rested for a decade. It was in 1922 that the British finally took a lead in telephone development and opened the first public exchange in the world which used automatic relays, at Fleetwood, in Lancashire.

At the end of the 1960s, the Post Office telephone monopoly was broken and private companies were allowed to market Private Automatic Branch Exchanges (PABX) above 100 lines, coinciding with great advances in the usage of the computer. Even more wonderful things began to take shape.

Let's look at just one, which affects the telephone answering machine.

One of the basic advantages of using the telephone is the fact that you have the undivided attention of the person at the other end of the line.

But how many times during this past week have you unsuccessfully tried to get through and speak to someone, failing because the lines were busy or the person was engaged elsewhere or just unavailable? How much did all this cost in terms of your time and possible lost business? Obviously, telephone answering machines partly solve the problem of unavailability, but only in a very limited way.

Soon they'll be outdated. By the year 2001, their only use will be for the consumer market.

'Voicebank', already operative for some years in San Francisco, and successfully installed in London, is a major technological step forward in this field. Voicebank is a computerized programme capable of processing text, data and voice information on a 'store and forward' basis.

With the inception of electronic mail, the Voicebank technique may be used as a 'voice note'. Recipients of the mail also receive advice that a voice note has been attached. The recipient then depresses a single key and will hear the originator's voice making comments. The full impact of the message will then be made, with no room for error or misunderstanding of the originator's intent.

After 70 years, the Post Office's telephone monopoly has been broken wide open. This has made a path for exciting growth, and all of us who are in business because we believe in the competitive free enterprise system know what is the natural sequel to competition: we'll be able to expect many more exciting developments by the end of this decade.

This poses a tremendous challenge to management.

In order to meet this era of telecommunications, management must be made aware that the traditional, face-to-face meeting in an initial stage of communication – and therefore of selling – is no longer necessary. In fact, it may even be termed obsolete.

The telephone in its present form is a time-saving, highly cost-effective tool. Used under specialist control – by professionals – the telephone must increase any company's profitability.

Here are 25 uses, each one practical, profitable and results-orientated:

1 As a substitute

When a geographical area becomes vacant through illness, vacation, or termination of employment of a salesperson, a regular telephone call to customers will keep the business 'live' and ensure that competitors won't creep in through the back door because of a lack of contact by your company.

2 Testing a mailing list

My experience of handling more than 1,500 computer files of major mailing lists shows that the telephone can be a very good testing ground for any such mailing list.

I have found that a good formula is 50 calls per 1,000 names and addresses. The use of the telephone is far cheaper than testing a list by means of a mailing, because of the lower quantity needed, and of course the answers come back much more quickly.

If, for example, you intended to rent a list purported to be of 250,000 parents with children under the age of five, or of detached house-owners, or companies owning main-frame computers, then the veracity and potential worth of that list can easily and speedily be checked by telephone.

3 Fund-raising

One of the first UK charities to understand the potential value of the telephone in terms of increased income was Dr Barnardo's Homes. Their training officer, John Kelson, became so involved in the successful use of the telephone as a fund-raising medium that he eventually became the first chairman of the telephone committee of the British Direct Marketing Association. It has been proved that the telephone is a very successful method of raising funds for any charity, institution, or other fundraising scheme, whether it involves selling tickets to a policeman's ball or direct contributions to building funds etc. One fairly large organization, for example, annually sells thousands of magazine subscriptions by telephone, after advising prospects that a percentage of the monies received is being donated to specific charities.

It is now not uncommon for businesses to receive at least one call a month asking them to sponsor a balloon race or a 20 mile walk on behalf of various good causes.

4 Test marketing

Where a good basic list is available, test marketing by telephone can be low-cost, flexible in terms of demographics, unbiased by person-to-person reactions, and very speedy.

An overseas manufacturer wished to launch his innovative water irrigation system in Denmark. The company had very little knowledge of the Scandinavian agricultural industry, but decided that before appointing agents it would be beneficial to have a detailed idea of the scope and need for the product.

A Danish telephone bureau was employed to make contact with 500 farmers owning large acreages. They were questioned on their existing methods of irrigation and their attitudes towards possible purchase of the new product. At the same time they were also asked to give details of the machinery agents whom they favoured when purchasing any new equipment.

Following the completion of this exercise, sufficient positive information was received to encourage the overseas manufacturer to make the necessary investment to launch the product. The next stage was the establishment of likely agencies, and using the information gained from the first exercise, a second telephone test marketing exercise was organized in which the possible prospective agents were asked various questions necessary in order to narrow the field sufficiently before the final choice was made. Upon completion of this second test, the results were analyzed and a third telephone marketing promotion was arranged in order to make firm qualified appointments with a short-list of likely candidates.

The managing director of the manufacturer then visited Denmark for two weeks and was able in this time to finalize his arrangements, having selected the agency with whom he wished to work.

Total cost of this test marketing before the launch of a new product was just £5,500. Had they not chosen to use the telephone, the operation could have been expected to involve an expenditure of around £15,000 with no guarantee that the end-result could not have been total failure.

Testing anything by telephone must make sense – demographic, pricing structure, geographical bias, product, timing, mailing list, or need.

Research comes into many test projects. For example, one manufacturer wished to test the market for a new, low-priced soft drink within a particular TV area. My company telephoned 500 confectionery retailers to ask if they would take part in a six-week survey during which they would be supplied with some outers of the soft drinks for display on their counters.

We explained what this entailed. Each week, these retailers would be telephoned and asked eight different market research questions; at the end of the six-week period each retailer who took part would receive £50 for his trouble (and of course be charged for the number of soft drinks actually sold). 405 retailers agreed to take part in the survey. Five 'dropped out' along the way and the remainder continued until the end of the scheme.

This telephone test marketing effort cost the manufacturer a total of £25,000. The same results, obtained in more conventional, old-fashioned ways, would probably have cost around £75,000 to £100,000.

5 Investigation

The speed of the telephone is phenomenal. There are some forms of investigation which can produce results in just one day when undertaken by telephone – that can make all the difference to a company's success or failure.

The case history which leaps to my mind is that of a multi-national electrical manufacturer with huge profits in all but one division of its group. This loss-making division was obviously a thorn in the side of management, and the directors issued instructions that the whole division would be closed down unless the situation was put right immediately.

The company's 'whizz-kid' was asked to look into the situation and it was he who approached my organization, asking us to contact 1,500 electrical wholesalers with the objective of discovering the reason why there was a drop in demand for what was, and is, an excellent product.

On the side, as it were, we were also told to note the requirements of any customer who wished to place an order. Finally, just before the campaign commenced, we were also told that the manufacturer had been about to launch a new (and as yet unnamed) electrical gadget onto the marketplace. Without any literature available, we were given a description of the product and its price and were asked to mention the gadget to the wholesalers.

The whole project took place in one day. The result was startling.

1,375 contacts immediately answered the company's basic question – why had the division lost its share of the marketplace? The answer was simple. The company had an inadequate salesforce, with an infrequent calling pattern. This fact had made it possible for the company's more aggressive competitors to take a larger slice of what was a fairly limited cake.

With the facts from these 1,375 reports available, our client therefore was able quickly to put matters right and bring the division back into profit fairly readily.

Interestingly, during the same exercise, we took in orders for the existing products totalling more than £10,000. And, as a bonus to a very successful and worthwhile exercise, we sold, sight unseen, a further £4,000 of the new product!

Yet the whole telephone campaign cost the manufacturer at that time (1979) only £1,500.

6   Testing campaign penetration

The telephone is a very capable ally in finding out the extent to which an advertising campaign has penetrated.

You may be heavily committed to large TV and print media budgets, and the results of these should soon be reflected in your sales, but until you know the extent of the penetration of your campaign, can you really be sure that the approaches adopted are giving you the best value for your money?

As a manufacturer of a washing-up liquid, does your product also appeal to farmers' wives and grandmothers? Are they even aware of your product? Has your advertising made its impact?

If you are a commercial stationers, advertising in all the trade journals, would it not be worthwhile finding out if your prospects are aware of your own inventory?

Testing the market isn't only useful for a company. It makes sense for any organization dealing with the public. One major British charity, in existence for more than a century, with an excellent management structure, comes to mind as an example. This highly respected organization undertakes much-needed family social work, both in visiting the homes of needy families (needy in the sense of emotional as well as financial support) and in the maintenance of homes for the aged. However, contributions had not been widely forthcoming from the community, and there appeared to be a certain lethargy towards this charity, despite the continuous educational advertisements which it placed in the relevant press.

My company made 500 telephone calls for this charity, asking questions along the lines of, 'Do you know what work this charity does?' and 'Is there a specific reason why you would not support it with contributions?'

Again, the answer became clear during the course of *just one evening* – the length of time it took us to conduct this campaign. The public was simply unaware of the extent of the charity's social work activities! Obviously, the charity's advertising had *not* succeeded in its objective – which was to educate.

The charity took the lesson to heart and began doing something about it, with success reflected in substantially higher donations.

7 Obtain qualified appointments

As I pointed out in Chapter 1, where I discussed the cost of keeping a salesman on the road, prospecting for qualified appointments by telephone makes good economic sense.

Finding examples is difficult, but only because the choice is so wide. I cannot think of any commercial or consumer direct-sell product or service sales of which cannot be cost-effectively increased by using the telephone to separate the good prospect from the time-waster with the representative being used solely to do the job for which he is employed – selling.

Take an everyday office need such as a photocopying machine. A hard-working salesman in a densely commercially-populated area could expect to sit in 12 waiting rooms every day, cooling his heels, and may be lucky enough to elicit interest from three prospects, who actually allow him to demonstrate his equipment. At the end of the week, from the 15 demonstrations, perhaps, he's lucky enough to get five sales.

If, however, his company had used the telephone on his behalf, then instead of 15 actual demonstrations resulting in five sales per week, he would have had 60 firm appointments with interested prospects during the same period. Eliminating time-wasting 'cold' calling, he could have made 20 sales.

The prospects would have been those people who had actually expressed an interest in having a new photocopier; each of them would have been prepared, well before the salesman's arrival, seriously to discuss the possibility of purchasing.

8 Repetitive selling

If you are selling the same product every week to the same customer list, be it cassette tapes, drink, confectionery, tobacco, ice cream or any merchandise, why waste the time of your sales force by converting them into order takers?

An example is provided by a multinational company which sells its products into do-it-yourself, hardware and paint shops, as well as into department stores. They analyzed their business and came to the conclusion that 90 per cent of it was repetitive selling. Their product was in fact the brand leader, a household name, and they had penetrated 80 per cent of all possible outlets.

After a considerable amount of testing, a training scheme was inaugurated for regional telephone sales supervisors, which was followed by the employment of about 100 home telephone owners. These people in turn were trained very thoroughly in the company's products and taught phoneselling. Each person now works from their own home, with a small microcomputer installation and very stringently-maintained reporting procedures. Within the first six months, sales rose by 35 per cent and subsequently continued upward. Because of the low cost of obtaining the sales by telephone, profit margins doubled.

9 Motivate lapsed accounts

Your very best prospect file is the one which has the names of your lapsed customers. What's happened to them? Has their business changed hands, and, if so, have the new owners been asked for their custom? Were they offended with something your company did, or had left undone – and has anything been done about smoothing things down? Have they been told about new lines, schemes, opportunities? Above all, has anyone actually asked why they no longer give you their custom? And does the customer know that their business is valued by your organization?

Good questions, I think you'll agree. Sadly, they're questions a lot of companies don't bother asking. And they're all questions which are easy to ask over the telephone.

That's something which a department store in France learned to its profit. It re-activated 42 per cent of all its lapsed account customers by telephoning to say the things we've just mentioned. Their campaign was linked to a special offer along the lines of 'A magnificent percolator will be sent free of charge if you place an order now, just to show how much we value your custom'.

Where resistance was met with, due to a real or imagined grievance from the past, this was dealt with speedily and professionally with the result that the account customer was once again committed to purchase from the store.

10   Preceding and/or following a direct mail campaign.

For companies involved in direct-mail campaigns, the telephone is an ideal 'insurance policy'. It should be used to precede the campaign and to qualify the company's prospect file, while at the same time updating and clarifying its mailing list. This eliminates the non-starters. The 'golden rule' here is don't send your expensive mailers to those who will never be your customers.

Use the telephone call to find out:

- If there is awareness of what you have to offer;
- Whether there's a possible need for your product/service;
- What company demographics would be applicable to your sales pitch;
- The name(s) of the decision-maker(s).

11 New launch

A vigorous promotion agency was asked to help in the launch of a new milk-based drink. This was aimed at the ten to twenties age group.

Some very striking advertising had been shown on Granada TV and the promotion agency was backing this with both direct mail and field sales selling face-to-face.

Because the initial consignment of the drinks was date-stamped, time was of the very essence in this launch – and the agency decided to use telephone marketing to follow through on the mailing campaign. Some 6,000 CTNs were contacted in the Granada TV area to coincide with the TV launch. The shops were asked to purchase some cases of the drinks in order to meet the demand which was being generated. As an added, but small incentive, a £1 discount was offered when two or more cases were purchased. Several tons of the product were sold in this way.

New products, schemes, colours, sizes or ideas can quickly and effectively be launched by telephone to a list of existing or peripheral customers.

'We want you to be one of the first to know that . . .' is a very positive approach which, by insinuation, combines flattery and education to produce a high level of orders – and all without incurring the costs inherent in face-to-face selling. This also applies, of course, to the promotion of special merchandise to generate store traffic.

These lessons don't only apply to big business. A well-known firm of portrait photographers in the USA specializing in family pictures provide another example. Many of them annually visit towns and villages, taking their cameras directly into the homes of their clients. Six weeks before their proposed visit, they habitually send a mailing to previous and prospective clients, enclosing a reply-paid card asking for convenient dates and times to be notified if the clients wish to have some photographs taken.

This horse-and-buggy approach worked successfully for several years until they decided to try the effect of a full scale phone-in, following a mailing to their previous prospective list file. The results were astonishing: their bookings increased substantially and the small but irritating percentage of non-fulfilled appointments almost disappeared.

12   Sale of surplus stock

A major distributor of toys who had the UK franchise for a well-known electronic game, undertook extensive TV and press advertising in the weeks prior to Christmas, in order to generate sales for the large volume of games due to be delivered at the beginning of November. To their horror an expected large consignment of the merchandise did not arrive as planned, but was belatedly delivered only on 15 December – too late for distribution in the normal way.

This meant that most of the stock would not be sold for some months, resulting in serious cash-flow problems for the company. The only solution was to contact 4,200 retailers very quickly, endeavouring to put forward a proposal attractive enough to encourage them to buy so near to Christmas.

Seventy telephone communicators were employed to contact the toy shops during the course of one day – 16 December. Each prospect was offered the inducement of a 'baker's dozen' – 13 games for every 12 ordered – as well as extended credit terms, with payments not being required until the end of January. Delivery was promised within two days, and the company's sales force was used to undertake this. By the end of 16 December, each piece of merchandise had been sold and was actually in the retail outlet by the 18th.

13   Converting enquiries to sales

How many advertisements actually attract your interest to such an extent that you fill in coupons and send for further information or samples, or both? And what happens after you have done so?

In most of the cases, you'll either place an order or not – it's as simple as that. Yet on those occasions when your enquiry is followed through by a telephone call in order to encourage and motivate you to proceed with a purchase, there is certainly a strong likelihood that you will do so.

The cost-effectiveness of this kind of promotion is dependent upon the product being offered and the seriousness of the original enquiry, and also the length of time which has elapsed before the follow-up contact is made.

All telephone marketing costs must be carefully monitored on an hourly basis, and particularly careful records should be maintained in order to develop the most effective pattern.

An example is provided by a passenger shipping line which produced a list of 1,800 people who in January 1982 had asked for details of the line's spring cruise. Their names were later checked against the ultimate passenger list, and those who were not taking part in the cruise were to be contacted in January 1983 and asked if they were still interested in a spring cruise.

180 telephone contacts, a random ten per cent of the total, revealed that the cost of following up after one year was *not* justified, and that the original enquiry had been made purely on impulse.

However, a tour operator specializing in winter sports who undertook exactly the same type of promotion found that the cost proved very justified – with an incredible 8.5 per cent of all those being contacted converting to firm bookings.

14   Incoming calls

Incoming direct orders and bookings must be taken just as professionally and controlled in the same way as any outgoing telephone campaign.

This applies whether the incoming telephone calls resulted from TV, radio, direct mail or point-of-sale advertising. Don't employ order-takers, but ensure that the telephones are answered by trained communicators able to perform their task – which is to sell, sell and sell.

Every opportunity is provided by this unique voice-to-voice situation to enable you to take advantage of the complete attention of the enquiree at the other end of the receiver. If the request is for a brochure, the communicator should, if this is relevant, give the address of the nearest stockist. Where an order is being placed, perhaps for a children's paddling pool, then the communicator ought also to try and sell swings, deckchairs, or whatever other items of this kind are stocked. If it is a retailer calling to order three cases of chocolate bars, then encourage the caller to buy nine or 12 cases by detailing the savings. Should the enquirer be interested in a service, holiday, insurance policy, private health scheme, then make sure the benefits are sold enthusiastically.

15 Inviting the prospect to a seminar

There are many larger items which cannot be sold without the benefit of a demonstration actually on site – but telephone selling is an excellent method of extending invitations to seminars, exhibitions and informative selling sessions.

One multinational computer manufacturer imaginatively organized a train to travel throughout Western Europe, stopping for two to three days in each major city, where their mainframe computer was demonstrated. Telephone marketers were used in each country two weeks prior to the scheduled visit in order to contact likely prospects, encourage interest wherever possible, and extend invitations to visit the exhibition at specific times.

Thousands of prospects took advantage of the proposal, and a very satisfactory level of sales was achieved, basically because the attendees in this instance all fell into one category of likely purchasers, certain parameters being established at the time of the original telephone call.

If, however, the invitations had been issued on an ad hoc basis throughout the usual media, there is no doubt that while the quantity of attendees might have been larger, the quality, in terms of definite prospects, would have been lower and the demonstrators' attention would have had to be spread thinly on the ground – with resultant fewer sales.

16 Political purposes

In the United States, telephone marketing has for many years figured very prominently in electioneering budgets and I have very little doubt that it will do so in the United Kingdom when next the country goes to the polling booths.

It is not unusual in America to receive a telephone call with a friendly voice saying out of the blue, 'Mr Brown? Hello there, the President would just like to say a few words to you about the election. . . .' This is then followed by a familiar (taped) voice giving the particular message.

154

Thousands of these combination live-and-taped calls are made daily and the response is said to be very satisfactory overall. The taped voice can be and often is that of a famous show business personality expounding the particular cause.

Taped messages of this kind are not only useful for political campaigns, but can be used to provide a testimonial for charities, products, services, holidays, real estate – in fact providing a method of motivating public opinion which can be used to promote virtually anything.

17 Direct selling

Anything from a £50 subscription to a £30,000 crane can be sold by telephone. I know – I've done it.

Providing the ground rules are followed carefully, direct sales can be concluded cost-effectively. It is particularly important to make the offer in a clear, honest and natural way – and to recapitulate by confirming in the exact instructions, so that the customer is absolutely sure of the terms and conditions relating to the sale.

In circumstances where the communicator is working on a commission basis, it is often advisable to use a verifier, whose job it is to qualify the sale. It would be unwise to convey to the client that a second call is being made for this specific purpose and verifiers should use gambits such as:

- 'We'd just like to confirm the delivery address.'
- 'Did we mention that you have a choice of colours?'
- 'Can I verify your name for invoice purposes?'

In view of the fact that it is undoubtedly easy for a prospect to place an order on the telephone which he or she may later repent, and possibly deny, it can save time and money if a verification call is made before the dispatch of a high-value order.

18 Mail order

When the *Daily Mail* decided to sell sweatshirts in aid of their *SAVE THE SEAL* appeal they used the services of my inbound telephone marketing company, who were able to not only take in orders for the sweatshirts, but also to invite callers to make a donation via their credit cards. An extraordinary sum of money was raised in this way. Any product can be sold using the telephone to take in and verify orders via credit card, and at the same time endeavouring to upsell on the original offer.

19 Dealer location

General Motors, with some of their models in short supply, were pleased to set up a dealer location service using the telephone to provide callers with up-to-the-minute information selling which dealers held stock of the various models. The service, which generated thousands of calls, saved time for would-be purchasers and resulted in additional goodwill towards the company for providing the efficient round-the-clock service.

20 Voting

Television stations, radios, newspapers and magazines all use telephone lines to register votes from their readers/listeners, either simple YES/NO to a particular problem – or more definitive answers. Unlike previous forms of polling, the total number of answers on each project is immediately known and can be published almost simultaneously.

21 Sales verification

Of particular relevance to mail order companies, using the telephone for sales verification makes a great deal of sense. Critics might say that it also gives purchasers the chance to re-think their original order, but this must be better than delivering goods only to have them returned. The same telephone call also gives the communicator a chance to explain the product, alter if an alternative is more efficient or even to upsell.

22 Converting customer service into sales

To convert an existing customer service department into a

productive telephone marketing centre, the communicators
need to be taught sales techniques. People who have already
established themselves as customers often want their loyalty re-
affirmed; and it is at this point that a good communicator can
convert them to become current accounts.

23 Providing product advice

Rather than complain, people who have bought a particular
product seek their revenge by 'bad-mouthing' the source of their
purchase, as well as no longer dealing with the company
concerned. This is the opportunity for a good product advice
centre where communicators can be trained to 'hand hold' and
develop a long-term relationship with customers.

24 Market research

Every market researcher should really bless the name of
Alexander Graham Bell. No longer is it always necessary to
stand on street corners and stop unwilling passers-by in order to
question them. The telephone and market research is a marriage
made in heaven. However small, every company needs research
on prospective buyers, product awareness and attitudes. Good
communicators can probe and obtain all information in a
controlled and careful manner.

25 Take-over bids and new issues

The great public share offers such as British Gas all made full use
of the telephone. Phone 'Sid' for a prospectus! – hundreds of
thousands of calls were made for this offer, and subsequent ones
for other major national industries. Companies seeking to ward
off take-over bids, acquire other companies or take certain
courses of action can immediately contact their shareholders by
telephone.

In telephone marketing you are joining an industry that is
continuously pushing the limits imposed by today's highly
competitive market. With Europe becoming one country,

telephone marketing is the quickest and most cost-effective way to identify a potential source of business overseas without the horrendous expense of setting up an office 'cold'.

By making a decision to use the telephone as a marketing tool, you will soon learn that there is almost no end to the ways in which the telephone can become your greatest asset in business, always providing that it is handled professionally and ethically, and given the time, the respect and the attention it deserves.

Index